Building Playgrounds, Engaging Communities

Louisiana State University Press)|(*Baton Rouge*

BUILDING PLAYGROUNDS, ENGAGING COMMUNITIES

Creating Safe and Happy Places for Children

Marybeth Lima

John David—
Thanks for your
commitment to service-
learning. Go play!

Yours in community,

Published by Louisiana State University Press
Copyright © 2013 by Louisiana State University Press
All rights reserved
Manufactured in the United States of America
First printing

Designer: Michelle A. Neustrom
Typeface: Museo Slab
Printer: McNaughton & Gunn, Inc.
Binder: Dekker Bookbinding

Library of Congress Cataloging-in-Publication Data

Lima, Marybeth, 1965–
  Building playgrounds, engaging communities : creating safe and happy places
for children / Marybeth Lima.
     pages cm
  Includes bibliographical references and index.
  ISBN 978-0-8071-4980-5 (cloth : alk. paper)—ISBN 978-0-8071-4981-2 (pdf)
—ISBN 978-0-8071-4982-9 (epub)—ISBN 978-0-8071-4983-6 (mobi) 1. Play-
grounds—Social aspects. 2. Playgrounds—Design and construction. I. Title.
  LB3251.L55 2013
  796.06'8—dc23

                                                                    2012027902

This book took a considerable amount of thought and represents the best of my heart. I thus dedicate it to the person who has stood with me and by me, head to head, heart to heart, and soul to soul since June 19, 1992: Lynn Erin Hathaway.

CONTENTS

Prologue / ix

1. How to Fit a Playground through the Back Door / *1*
2. You Can't Make a Playground Gumbo without the Ladies / *18*
3. Playgrounds Rule and Playground Rules / *36*
4. Triumphing over Murphy's Law on Steroids / *60*
5. Community Stone Soup: Breaking the Myth of "Broken" Schools / *88*
6. A Brief Survival Guide for Community Engagement Marathons / *106*
7. Getting Involved: Advice from Community Fire Plugs / *132*

   Epilogue / *154*

Appendix 1: Information on Playground Safety / 159

Appendix 2: Volunteer Organizations / 166

Note on Sources / 169

Acknowledgments / 175

Index / 181

Illustrations follow page 105

PROLOGUE

I am a professor in biological and agricultural engineering at Louisiana State University, and I have the best job on the planet. I came to Louisiana in the fall of 1996, in the middle of a U.S. Senate race that pitted Mary Landrieu against Woody Jenkins. The charged campaign, narrow victory by Landrieu, and ensuing furor over alleged election fraud introduced me to Louisiana politics and colorful characters from the start.

My beginnings at LSU were far less charged, but for me, just as interesting. I have been conducting research and teaching classes in biological engineering since that fall of 1996. I came to Louisiana by way of Columbus, Ohio, and Ohio State University, and with me I brought a huge dose of earnestness (Midwesterners have the market cornered on earnestness) and a burning desire to transform engineering education from the production of highly skilled barbarians to the creation of holistic problem solvers.

In the spring of 1997, I was assigned to teach a first-year biological engineering design course. My initial goal was to have students work in groups to design something "real" that they would find interesting. This goal led me to the use of service-learning, a method of teaching in which students master their learning objectives by working with a community partner to address a critical community need. A committed group of people on and off the LSU campus helped me develop an idea to focus on public school playground design for this course, and to involve the community and their expertise in the design process. This collaboration developed into a program called the LSU Community Playground Project.

The process of designing and building community playgrounds is not extraordinary in and of itself. Much of the construction process involves killing grass, moving dirt, and other mundane activities. Ask a playground construction volunteer who has just spent an entire day placing engineered wood fiber or another suitable playground safety surfacing material under and around play equipment, and you will be treated to an earful about the mundane.

Although many of the activities around designing and building playgrounds can be routine, the process of working with community is anything but. This book is organized into two main parts. The first contains the collective stories of people and communities as we have worked together to ensure that every child in the local public school system has access to a safe, fun playground that the kids themselves helped to design, and the second focuses on larger issues involving community, including how to get involved in your own community and how to make your efforts sustainable over time.

The LSU Community Playground Project has taken me on a fantastic journey with people and to places I would never have traveled otherwise, and it is why I have the best job on the planet. I hope you enjoy reading this book as much as I enjoyed writing it.

Building Playgrounds, Engaging Communities

You're not going to give up on us now, are you?
—Georgia Jenkins

How to Fit a Playground through the Back Door

My heart pounded in my throat, and I could feel the blood rushing through my ears. The twelve laughing children were suspended in air, defying gravity as they gripped the steering wheel and railings of the model fire truck, which balanced precariously at a 45-degree angle from the ground. "Turn!" the leader shouted, and the other children shifted their weight starboard in one smooth motion, bringing the truck back down to the earth with a metal against concrete crash that reminded me a little of nails on a chalkboard. I was watching "Put Out the Fire," the favorite game of the children of Beechwood Elementary School, on their favorite piece of play equipment. As the children bounced along on the spring-loaded truck, I could hear chatter between the "radio" and the driver, while the kids gripping the railings let go to begin putting on imaginary fire gear. "ETA five minutes!" the driver yelled back to his firefighters. "Pull left!" The children grabbed the railings again and leaned toward port as the large metal fire truck vaulted onto two wheels to take a fast corner in slow motion. The smiles on the children's faces showcased their confidence and sense of adventure; my pounding heart and clenched jaw betrayed my concern for their safety.

My presence at Beechwood was completely arbitrary. When I was in graduate school, I was lucky to befriend Mary Sansalone, a civil engineering professor who was the faculty advisor of the Cornell University civil engineering student club. One of the students in this club had designed a playground, and Mary had assisted the student in making the design a club service project. I participated in a day of service for building that playground, which was constructed at a local school. The project stuck in my mind, and when I considered projects for my first-year engineering students to undertake as part of their engineering design experience, I thought about playgrounds. Their appeal is universal, and virtually everyone is familiar with them; I thought that a playground design could be moved into the classroom as a project. I shared these ideas with a group of friends over dinner one night, and upon hearing my thoughts, Ramona Patterson jumped up from her chair and said, "I am a teacher at Beechwood Elementary School and you can do our school playground! Wait until you see it, the kids really need a new playground."

I visited Beechwood for the first time in the fall of 1998. The first place I went on the school campus was the first place one should always go when visiting a school: the front office. There, I met Georgia Jenkins, the principal at Beechwood. Principal Jenkins should be on the poster for outstanding school leaders; she was competent, professional, and had the best interests of all 325 children at Beechwood in mind and in heart. She was a master at "time on task" and at simultaneously keeping a tight ship while providing a nurturing environment for her students.

Georgia gave me a tour of the classrooms during instruction and of the playground during recess. She informed me that the playground had been built in 1960, the same year that the school was constructed. The playground was then thirty-eight years old, six years older than I was at the time, and much worse for the wear. It was during this visit that I saw the children play "Put Out the Fire" for the first time. My heart-stopping nervousness was appropriate. I learned later, in playground safety school, that impact failures, in which equipment falls on top of children, were one of the main reasons that children are killed on playgrounds. Luckily, this never happened at Beechwood.

I made a couple of more visits to Beechwood in the fall of 1998, meeting the teachers and some of the students; we planned when my students would come to meet with Beechwood students to start designing a playground. We were careful to work around the children's school schedules so that the children would receive maximal instruction but would also have a chance to interact with my students to talk shop about play and playgrounds.

The semester started in January 1999. I stood up on the first day of class and told my students, "This semester, we're going to design a playground with a local public school. I don't know how to design a playground right now, but we're going to learn together." I taught my students about engineering design; I also searched the literature for information on playground design and synthesized this information into lessons a day before I taught it to my students. The children at Beechwood shared all their ideas about play, including what they actually did on the playground and what they hoped to do on a new playground.

Beechwood students taught my students how to play "King of the Tire," which is the same thing as "King of the Hill," but in which the winner stood on top of a partially sunken old tire in the ground instead of on an actual hill. The Beechwood students wanted a place to swing and to slide; they could do neither in their current playground. Georgia, assistant principal Laura East, and the teachers at Beechwood provided additional guidance. "This may not look like much of a playground to you," they told my students, "but to these kids, it is everything they have and they are proud of it. Do everything you can to keep all this equipment. Add to what we have, don't take anything away. If what we have is not safe, make it safe. Remove it only as a last resort." I taught my students about active play places and passive play places, and how having both on a playground is critically important to provide children with a variety of opportunities to experience different kinds of play, whether it involves running around, climbing, and playing games like "Put Out the Fire" or "King of the Tire," or whether it involves storytelling and watching butterflies in the garden.

My students created three playground design concepts based on basic information about engineering design and playgrounds provided by me, dynamic knowledge about play and the playful spirit from the Beechwood children, and the twin mandates of safety and sustainability given by the Beechwood teachers and administrators. When my students presented these playground design concepts to the Beechwood kids, they received very specific feedback: "We love the spiral slide. We hate that climber. We want that playhouse under our oak tree. Change the color of that wheel from yellow to red," and so on. My students changed their playground design concepts in response to Beechwood student input, wrote up their final reports, completed their playground drawings, and submitted them to me for a grade. The semester ended.

When I received my teaching evaluations (anonymously filled out by my students) a few weeks after the end of the semester, the highest score I received (3.9/4.0)—higher than "student interest was generated in the subject matter," "instructor encouraged questions and answered them clearly," and "student reactions were given consideration"—was "instructor thoroughly understood the subject matter." I was surprised, since I'd announced on the first day of class that I didn't know how to design a playground—that is, I *didn't* know the subject matter, much less thoroughly know it. I thought about this anomaly and came to the conclusion that I had received a high score on this metric because I modeled how to learn to design a playground instead of just how to design a playground. The importance of teaching students "how to learn" in addition to "how to" was a critical lesson for me as a young teacher. Teaching students the conceptual framework of how to learn, in addition to the techniques that they learn, remains a core aspect of my teaching philosophy to this day.

In May 1999, I had three possible playground designs for Beechwood Elementary sitting on my desk. I brought the reports to Beechwood and began working with the School Improvement Team (SIT), which was comprised of Beechwood teachers, administrators, and parents, to combine the three possibilities into one consolidated design. We finished this process in several months, after the SIT conferred with the children, teachers, physical education teacher, principal, assistant principal, and parents about which parts of each design should be included in the final playground. Our dream playground design featured a composite structure with a spiral slide, a wave slide, an arch climber, a tic-tac-toe board, a steering wheel, and a ladder. We also added a swing set, a playhouse, and a series of tunnels. We planned to refurbish the fire truck and big geodesic dome by adding paint, shortening bolts that were too long (and were thus entanglement hazards), and ensuring that the springs in the fire truck were properly attached to the concrete slab below. We planned to leave the sunken tires in place and buy a new tether ball for the tether pole, as well as basketball nets and basketballs for the existing court. Finally, we planned to place playground safety surfacing, known as "surfacing" for short, under and around all the playground equipment. Playground safety surfacing is a soft material that breaks falls and is a critical part of having a safe playground so that kids do not sustain life-threatening head injuries if they fall to the ground from elevated playground equipment. The new design was going to cost at least $30,000.

We had no money to build the playground, so the next order of business was to figure out how to get it. Georgia Jenkins leaned on me for this part of the process, so I started writing proposals to fund the new playground. Georgia never let me forget her school, not once. She called me like clockwork every two months, saying "You're not going to give up on us, are you?" The SIT provided guidance and told me that the math and science magnet program at Beechwood could be a hook for potential funders if we could figure out a way to link the magnet program with the playground. The magnet program was a source of pride for the school, but it was also a potential stress; one SIT member bluntly informed me that Beechwood would not be able to keep the magnet program if the school couldn't attract more white students to enroll in it.

I started writing proposals for the Beechwood playground and started getting rejections immediately. A small grant, in the $1,000 range, led to my students and Beechwood students building a butterfly garden and bird sanctuary at the school, but bigger grants that could fully fund the playground remained elusive.

I wasn't giving up, but I was still learning the ropes of proposal writing as an early-career assistant professor. I learned quickly through trial and error that many organizations would not fund equipment or infrastructure, and I wrote several more unsuccessful proposals to fund the Beechwood playground.

On my fifth or sixth try, I finally got funded by a Louisiana Board of Regents program called LaCEPT, an acronym which stands for "Louisiana Collaborative for Excellence through the Preparation of Teachers." Although funding for LaCEPT no longer exists, this program was immensely helpful to me because it put me in touch with a number of faculty members from around the state who were conducting research on best practices for STEM (Science, Technology, Engineering, and Mathematics) educators in K–12 and higher education settings.

I worked in this collaborative and with the teachers at Beechwood (especially magnet educator Lois LeDuff) to develop a mini-curriculum for elementary school students to learn about math and science while on a playground. Measurement was an important concept for fourth-graders, so we developed a unit on playground measurements and why they are important. The type of equipment on a playground—for example, climbers and swings—is used to determine the use zone around this equipment. The use zone is the area under and around play equipment in which a child who falls from the equipment is likely to land. We could teach fourth-graders how to determine the use zone of various types of play equipment using measurement, highlighting the calculation of perimeter and area. Measuring the height of the equipment will provide one with the depth of surfacing needed within the use zone, so students could figure out the volume of material needed, and so on.

Thus, the playground for Beechwood was funded through the back door. We didn't get the grant to build the playground; we got the grant to develop the playground curriculum. If the sum total of our efforts in curriculum development led to the construction of a playground—the outdoor learning environment in which we could execute the play curriculum—then we fully met the project objectives of the grant. This was another important lesson for me as a young faculty member: the idea that some projects could be funded in a straightforward manner, while others took a little creative framing. I have used this concept so many times in the ensuing years of community-based playground design and building that I often feel like I live through the back door.

With grant money in hand, I proceeded to butcher my way through the LSU bid process, not intentionally, but due to the fact that my previous training had not encompassed writing bid specifications, which tell a company exactly what is needed on a project. After many iterations on the bid document, LSU finally published the bid solicitation so that playground manufacturing companies could compete to provide the materials for our playground, as well as the supervision for our student volunteers who would build it. Although our design was unique, we planned to build the playground with prefabricated components supplied by a playground manufacturing company in order to minimize liability. A small, family-owned, local company named Agrestics got the bid. Just as Georgia Jenkins belongs on the "awesome school principal" poster, Agrestics belongs on the "taking pride in your hard work" poster.

I worked with Agrestics to get the equipment components ordered and with Beechwood to determine our build days. At this point, I was also staying up at night thinking to myself, "How can we guarantee the safety of 325 kids a day, 182 days a year, plus the safety of all the neighborhood kids 365 days a year?" (Beechwood, like most public schools, shared its playground with the local community.) Luckily, knowledge is power, and I was learning more about playgrounds all the time. Agrestics personnel and further research provided me with enough information to end my sleepless nights. While we can't guarantee that no one will ever be hurt on a playground, with proper maintenance of playground equipment, constant compliance with playground safety recommendations, and proper adult supervision, we can minimize serious injuries on playgrounds.

When I approached my students about volunteering to build the Beechwood playground, I was pleasantly surprised by their interest and enthusiasm. Many of the thirty-seven students who had been involved in the initial playground design volunteered because they were eager to participate in a process that would take their designs on paper to designs in reality. Many other biological engineering students also volunteered; by the end of the build, almost half of our 130 majors had spent at least four hours at the site. Twelve of my students came out almost every day, for ten hours a day, without fail. So did four of the students from Beechwood who lived in the neighborhood. Build hours were 7 a.m. to 5 p.m. Monday through Friday for two weeks, with the second weekend thrown in for final touches. My partner Lynn was also on the playground site full-time; she had moved from Columbus, Ohio, ten days before the build began, thankfully ending the long-distance chapter in our relationship.

We began our work on July 31, 2000. Kenny, the construction foreman from Agrestics, was our fearless leader during the build. He was also a character. Think Jack Nicholson, add twenty pounds, and take away absolutely no attitude. For the first three days of the build, all of us were working on the same thing: digging holes with post hole diggers, or PhDs. There are no PhDs (doctors of philosophy) on a playground site other than post hole diggers. Anyone with a PhD on a playground site must check their degree credentials and their egos at the door. Playground building is a time for flat-out working hard with your hands, your heart, and every ounce of strength and brawn that you possess; degree credentials are meaningless in this context.

We sweated and slogged those first three days, working entire mornings to dig about four inches into the soil, as Baton Rouge was experiencing a rare but significant drought. We took breaks in the shade of oak trees, drinking gallons of water from big plastic water dispensers. Every single day at lunchtime, Georgia Jenkins and Laura East would provide lunch to the volunteers, either out of their own pockets or courtesy of a group of neighborhood women whose children went to the school and/or attended the local church. Every day we were treated to a full spread. My students and the Beechwood students worked hard, but we were all fed well and encouraged to keep going by Georgia, Laura, and the neighborhood ladies, who lavished us with equal portions of food and support during the lunch hour.

On the fourth morning, we were digging holes in the ground for the large composite structure when two students called me over and said, "Hey, Doc, look at this! Pink concrete! It's kind of pretty. We're chipping through some of it. What do you think it is?" I was admiring the pretty color when Kenny came on the run, his ancient penny loafers beating across the sidewalk. He reached us and puffed, "STOP DIGGING."

I didn't know it at the time, but red concrete (as it is known) means danger; it is used to enclose power lines that can carry up to two millions volts of electricity. Despite the fact that we had dutifully contacted Louisiana One Call, which is required when digging to identify the location of all power, sewer, water, and gas lines so you won't dig into them, and despite the fact that Lousiana One Call had in turn dutifully marked all our lines beforehand and we were digging well away from them, we had located lines that were not on any map. We filled in the hole and, on the fly, had to move the play equipment we were planning to install in that location to another location. Kenny earned his pay every day, but especially on that day, when he saved us from potential disaster.

After four full days of digging, Agrestics decided to dispense with the slow way and rented a Bobcat for digging the holes we had not yet finished. Although the rental of this machine meant that Agrestics received less money for the build portion of the project, it sped our progress immensely.

On the seventh day of building, I was wearing an old pair of cut-off jeans and split them open while bending down to scoop dirt out of a hole. I pulled my T-shirt down over my split pants the rest of the day and learned the embarrassing way that material like denim is not conducive to playground builds during hot weather—its propensity to stick to your body because of sweat is sometimes greater than its ability to move in response to your body. I've never again worn jeans on a construction site in the summer and have never again split open my pants on a work site.

Throughout the two-week build, I was struck by the egalitarian nature of the construction process. Agrestics provided a strong example for everyone in this context; Belinda, Kenny's niece, knew as much about construction as Kenny did. Playground volunteers weren't chosen for particular jobs because of gender or experience, but for other reasons, such as whoever happened to be within arm's reach of Kenny or Belinda. In my case, because I am the approximate size of a fifth-grader, they'd put me on top of decks when first placed against support posts to fasten hardware from the top. Since volunteers had to support my weight plus the weight of the deck, being little made me ideal for such a job.

Although I'd used a hammer before, I was no construction expert. During this period, I learned how to mix and pour concrete, how to build sturdy wood borders to contain surfacing, and how to use a ram set, a tool which drives nails through concrete. I also learned about the second half of the 80/20 rule. The 80/20 rule says that you get 80 percent of a project done in 20 percent of the time, and that the last 20 percent of the project—the details—takes 80 percent of the time. I am pretty good at the 80 percent part of the rule, stopping a project when I deem something good enough; the 20 percent part reminds me of perfectionism territory, a place I don't often venture, especially in outdoor, physical work and construction, building-type projects. Agrestics made their living with the 80 percent part of the Beechwood construction job; they created their sense of purpose and showed their great care in their work in the remaining 20 percent. It is because of Agrestics and the Beechwood playground build that I now go for 100 percent of any job as much as I can. There are worlds of difference between "good enough" and "great."

The construction of the Beechwood playground reminded me of a regular construction site, with lots of people doing fairly mundane things for a long time and the sum total of our work looking like nothing much was happening. But like a regular construction site, once we got all the holes dug and the equipment unwrapped and hardware organized, the playground went up FAST. We felt so accomplished when the equipment was up and the surfacing containment zones were built. That process took eight days.

Then it was on to two straight days of surfacing, which involved unpacking mulch from bags packaged by the pallet, cutting them open with box cutters (pre 9/11, when a box cutter was just a box cutter), and dumping the surfacing throughout the play area. On the second day of surfacing, which was the Friday before school started, Georgia Jenkins brought out all her teachers to help. It was a scene close to bedlam, with the thirty or so of us, the thirty Beechwood teachers, and a crush of children working together; somehow, all the kids in the neighborhood found out about the action at Beechwood and came to hang out and work with us. Having all the extra hands made short work of the job; the collective excitement of the neighborhood made the task joyful.

We worked through the weekend to make sure that the playground was ready. On Sunday morning, Belinda carefully went over the composite structure, the playhouse, the swings, the tunnels, and all the equipment we'd refurbished to make sure that there were no sharp edges and no pinch points. Lynn and I sanded wood edges, tightened all the hardware, and raked the surfacing until it was perfectly, and I mean perfectly, level.

I was not at Beechwood for the morning of the first day of school, but the teachers told me later that the kids were absolutely elated with their new playground. I don't know how they kept the kids away from the playground that first morning, but they managed to do so. Lunchtime brought a dedication ceremony that the school had planned; it was a first-class deal, with refreshments and great fanfare. A member of the city council and a reporter from the local newspaper were present. Many of the volunteers came, everyone from Agrestics was there, and people from the Lousiana Board of Regents LaCEPT program came to show their support. Dignitary-type talk was kept to a minimum because the din of excited children sitting on the sidewalks surrounding the play area was so palpable. Georgia spoke briefly about the process and invited me to the center of the playground, where she handed me a pair of garden shears and told me to cut the ribbon. The school had etched a "thank you" into those shears—they hang in my office to this day. Once I had cut the ribbon and the adults had moved out of the way, Georgia called, "Go!" through her microphone, and the kids rushed that playground like holiday shoppers entering a Target store at 5 a.m. on black Friday. I can still hear their squealing and whooping.

Watching those kids attack the Beechwood playground that they had had a hand in designing evoked a feeling like none I had ever had. It wasn't about pride, though I was proud of the work, and it wasn't about happiness, though happiness pervaded every molecule of the Beechwood ether that day. It was the knowledge that every person involved in the playground project gave something to the community, and that something would keep on giving for as long as the playground lives. Everyone gave something positive, and all that giving will continue to multiply and spin off in ways that are easy to see and in ways that are not, but that collectively result in a boundless, affirming energy that can and does change the world.

On the dedication day of the Beechwood playground, I felt accomplished. I heaved a huge sigh of relief because the playground was finally finished after two years of hard work. I was done, and it was over. And it was over, for one week, until the principal of Villa del Rey Elementary called and asked if we could do a playground at her school. Our local newspaper had published an article on the Beechwood playground, and enterprising principals are always on the lookout for ways to improve their schools. I met with the Villa del Rey principal and committed to a new playground design project for my next batch of first-year engineering students in the spring.

As it turned out, I wasn't done with Beechwood either. Georgia asked me to join the SIT, and for the next two years, I worked with teachers and parents on issues that affected the school. There were small issues, such as trying to raise money for teacher appreciation days, and larger issues, such as the school's magnet program. Beechwood eventually lost this program, ostensibly because they couldn't attract enough white children to the school for it.

One day, a parent came to speak with the SIT; a crack house had recently been established two blocks from the school, and the parent's little girl had to walk past the place every day on her way home from school. The parent asked the SIT to figure out ways to get her little girl home safely each day. Both she and the girl's father worked full-time and couldn't walk their daughter home, and the police couldn't commit to a daily escort. I watched as teachers immediately volunteered to take turns walking the child past the house. I learned a great many things from working with the Beechwood community; that day, the teachers at Beechwood taught me courage.

I met a man named Joe Howell shortly after the Beechwood dedication ceremony; he was the new grounds and maintenance manager for Aramark, the company that the public school system subcontracted with to provide these services for the schools. Joe told me that he was committed to playground safety, but it wasn't until years later that I found out why: his ten-year-old daughter had broken her arm on a set of monkey bars that had had no protective surfacing. As a result, he made it his personal mission to make sure that all the play equipment in the school system was surfaced properly. Joe told me that if I ever decided to build another playground in the school system and could come up with the money to purchase the play equipment, he would find the money for playground safety surfacing. It is a promise that he has always kept, despite the fact that it sometimes has taken creative budgeting.

A year after installing the Beechwood playground, I took my new crop of first-year biological engineering students, the ones working on the Villa del Rey playground, to the Beechwood playground for a tour. The teacher giving us the tour walked by one of the benches under an oak tree and told the group, "We are so glad that y'all put that bench right there! When our kids are bad, we make them sit on the bench and watch their classmates while they're all playing on the playground and having fun. That bench has been a very effective tool for making sure our that kids behave!"

This experience was my first lesson in unintended consequences. During the design phase, my students had been very deliberate about placement of benches throughout the playground, and the bench the teacher mentioned was in an ideal location for passive play. What we intended as a play place was being used as a place of punishment instead. And that's fine—communities make it work for themselves in the best possible way, which is how it should be.

In 2003, Baton Rouge settled a lawsuit with the U.S. Department of Justice involving the desegregation of public schools. At the time, the 47-year-old lawsuit was the longest running of its kind in the country. When the dust settled, the paperwork was signed, and the schools were officially declared desegregated, four Baton Rouge public elementary schools were closed. Beechwood was one of them. Its last day of operation was in May 2005. We had designed the playground to last twenty years—it served the Beechwood community for almost five.

Joe Howell carefully removed the equipment at the Beechwood playground the following year and reinstalled it at another school, teaching my students another important lesson in sustainability. Joe chose the school that he felt was in the greatest need, and the composite structure and playhouse are now serving children at Jefferson Terrace Elementary School. He didn't reinstall the swings because even with their great thickness, the wood support posts we used didn't hold up to heavy use; the beloved fire truck and "King of the Tire" tires didn't make it either. Joe told me later that when he was in the process of moving the Beechwood playground equipment, five principals were fighting with each other over who would get it. Given the way that teachers and principals tended to cooperate and collaborate, the conflict spoke volumes about the need for playground equipment.

The playground at Beechwood Elementary School is emblematic of the entire process of the LSU Community Playground Project. A lot of mistakes, a ton of heart, and the combined efforts of about five hundred people—most of whom were children—went into this project. We experienced unintended consequences along the road, every person involved learned something new, and the playground that we worked so hard to create no longer exists in its current form.

Beechwood was a long time ago. In the ensuing years, I have worked with numerous community partners to repeat the playground design process more than thirty times, and our work together has resulted in the construction of more than twenty-five playgrounds. A lot of things have changed. The number of students majoring in biological engineering has more than tripled from the time I started my faculty career, and the size of my playground design class has increased dramatically as a result. Georgia retired. Agrestics partnered with us on several more playground builds before shutting their doors when the president of the company retired.

The playground that took us twelve days to build in the year 2000 now takes approximately two days, as we learned how to make playground builds more efficient. There are no longer any children allowed on the playground construction site for liability reasons. We never use wood as a playground building material; we use coated metal as much as possible because it is much more durable.

We've gone about making the playground design process more systematic; the collaboration among the local public school system, Joe and Aramark, and the LSU Community Playground Project has resulted in a concerted effort to make all public school playgrounds safe, fun, accessible, and modern. Joe had several of his employees train to become Certified Playground Safety Inspectors (CPSIs). They inspect all area schools every one to two years and provide me and the school system with a list of school playgrounds in order of need for improvement. Accordingly, I choose which schools my playground design class will collaborate with from this list of schools. Our local public school playgrounds are safer because Joe has surfaced every single piece of usable equipment in the public school system. Additionally, many of the schools have new play equipment thanks to our collective work together.

Schools' interest in improving their playgrounds has changed as well. What began as a trickle of interest with Villa Del Rey Elementary has led to a spiraling need for new playgrounds inside and outside East Baton Rouge Parish that continues to this day. To address this need, I hire students who show particular interest and aptitude in working with community and playgrounds to be part of the playground research and design team. Many of these students have also become CPSIs. We work year round with schools to develop designs, write bid specifications, and plan community playground builds. My focus with the playground project has become chasing money. I am no longer a young assistant professor learning the ropes of proposal writing and being mistaken for an undergraduate student. I am a seasoned veteran, cranking out proposals for playground funding as fast as I can get to them; with my gray hair, I am in the words of Paul Simon, sailing on silver. I am never mistaken for an undergraduate.

Although much has changed, some things have stayed the same. The feeling I get when I see children letting loose on their new playground for the first time is every bit as rich and transformative as it was at Beechwood. Likewise, my passion for justice is as strong now as it was when I started.

Like many good endeavors, the LSU Community Playground Project began by accident. I did not set out to do all the public school playgrounds in my local community; I set out to do one. I started the Beechwood playground project with positive outcomes in mind primarily for my students. Since then, my sphere has expanded to positive outcomes for everyone, with my students as only one part of an entire symphony of players necessary to learn and teach together to address a critical community need: a child's right (not a child's privilege) to a safe, fun, accessible, community-designed playground.

Access to a playground may seem like a tiny thing, a thing that many of us take for granted. In far too many of our communities in the United States and beyond, children either do not have access to playgrounds or else have access to playgrounds that are not well maintained or supervised. Playground accidents are the second most frequent reason that kids go to the emergency room every year in the United States, with an average of over 200,000 emergency room visits a year (bike accidents are the first, with about 300,000 emergency room visits a year). Some children do not have access to playgrounds by virtue of where they live; others have geographical access to playgrounds but not wheelchair access. Many have access to playgrounds that are not in compliance with safety guidelines. Some kids only have access to their school playgrounds, and sometimes school playgrounds are nonexistent. Access to play may seem like a tiny thing, but to me, it feels like everything.

You Can't Make a Playground Gumbo without the Ladies

The secret to good playground design—and really any kind of design—is knowing, understanding, and embracing the people who will use it. The true experts in play are children; the true experts in the community that the playground will serve are the members of the community. Experts in playground design, playground installation, playground safety, and child-hood development are necessary to ensure that the playground is safe, fun, accessible, and appropriate. The experts in playground maintenance are the people who are trained and experienced in this area. The experts in using the playground after it is built are children and professionals in child development and physical education. Input from all of these groups is critical for my college students who are starting their journeys to become proficient in engineering design.

My student Brian Etier summed it up well when asked by a community partner what he learned from the playground design experience. He said, "I learned about the importance of perspective in engineering. I had to think like a child to design the best playground. I had to think like a parent to design a safe playground. I had to think as a member of the community to design a playground that reflected the unique aspects of the community. I had to think like a politician to sell the playground to potential funders."

People are the key to everything. The work I have done with Baton Rouge and surrounding communities, mostly through public schools but also through organizations that serve children with special needs and organizations that serve survivors of hurricanes, has taught me so much more than play, history, and community relationships. Working with people, all kinds of people, representing very different perspectives, has taught me that differences are a fount of collective creative wisdom, that listening is an art that requires all five of your senses, and that taking pride in your community is an act that creates a living, breathing thing. A school is a living, breathing thing. So is a playground. And it is people who make it so.

The people involved in the LSU Community Playground Project generally fall into four categories: the play experts (the children), the school staff (teachers and administration), my students, and other community members and players in the process. Here's a deeper look at the people who together create a little slice of heaven in my community.

Children: The Sparks

Children are by far the biggest contingent in the playground design process. I have interacted with approximately 11,000 children in the context of playground design. As a group, kids are fantastic to work with because they freely share their ideas, dreams, and opinions—and not just about playgrounds. You're just as likely to hear about siblings, Harry Potter, Zelda, or Spiderman as you are the games that the kids have created and regularly play, or the awesome obstacle course that Coach (the inevitable name for a good physical education teacher) organized last week during recess.

Kids tell us all about play through their drawings, their writings, and through conversations. Some express basic wishes, like having a football or basketball or hula hoop to play with during recess. Sometimes the infusion of $500 to a school for these types of items transforms the play space and recess. In those cases, when you start with an open field that contains nothing, adding these types of items (called manipulatives) provides a platform for many types of play.

Many kids express an interest in play equipment similar to that which they've experienced before in other places, such as swings, slides, monkey bars, soccer goals, and interactive gardens. Other kids have more elaborate ideas. Common themes along this line of creative thinking include a pool with a whale in it, a roller coaster and/or amusement park, a video game arcade, and a large penned space for the family pets to come to school and interact with their friends and their friends' pets. Oh, and LSU's live tiger mascot Mike is welcome to visit this penned space at any time.

Some children remain indelibly etched into my consciousness. One early, defining moment in my playground travels occurred when a teacher at Villa Del Rey Elementary asked a student who was blind if it was okay for me to touch his forehead. When he assented, she said to me, "Run your fingers across his forehead." I did, and as I felt the pocks and ridges in the bone beneath his skin, she said, "Can y'all design something that he can run around on without breaking his head open?"

During one initial visit to a school in which my college students spoke with elementary school students for the first time, as everyone was filing into the cafeteria for a playground rap session, a little girl put her hands on her hips and, with a very tough look on her face, demanded, "What are all you white people doing here?" After about an hour of drawing, conversation, and college student note-taking, we were all filing out of the cafeteria when the same little girl announced, with the same very tough look on her face (but without hands on hips), "You know, you white people are okay."

The fourth playground we completed was at McMains Children's Developmental Center, the cerebral palsy center for greater Baton Rouge. The children who received therapy at McMains had access to excellent indoor facilities, but their outdoor playground had been built in 1954 and was not wheelchair accessible. My biological engineering students worked with the children and staff affiliated with McMains to design the playground while LSU English instructor Deb Normand's technical writing students worked with McMains executive director Janet Ketcham to write a successful $50,000 grant to fund the remainder of the playground. At the celebration ceremony, Deb came up to me and pointed out a little girl who was making her way up the stair unit of a composite structure and was on her way to a slide. Deb told me that a McMains staff member had just informed her that this little girl had been unable to walk prior to the construction of the playground. The staff member said that the little girl was so excited about the new playground and was so determined to get onto that composite structure to play that she learned to walk. She now negotiated the entire structure, not with ease, but with resolve and with joy.

Principals and teachers also hear zingers from children that can cut to the bone, in good ways and in difficult ones. A principal who had described bedlam on her campus, with her entire student body upset because a condemned piece of beloved playground equipment had been removed, called me two weeks after new playground we designed together had been finished. She reported that she had been watching the children play on the new playground when a first-grader ran up to her and asked, "Can we keep it?"

Cindy Murphy, a teacher who has been working diligently for three years on procuring a new playground for Wildwood Elementary, told me that on the first day of school, she was supervising children during recess when a little girl who had just entered pre-kindergarten walked up to her and asked, "Is this all you got?" Cindy felt like it was pointless to explain that she was working on getting new playground equipment at the school and told me later she felt terrible, but she looked that little girl straight in the eye and answered, "Yes, baby, this is everything we have right now."

While individual kids have left deep impressions upon me, groups of children have done the same. One of the hardest things I've ever witnessed was a group of kids on the day that their school playground equipment was taken away. Even if play equipment is dangerous, the kids who play on that equipment love it and have an attachment to it. If you are going to remove something from their playground, you should be ready to add something immediately, because the trauma of losing a playground is huge and immediate. Too many principals have shared horror stories with me about hoards of crying children pressing against chain-link fence and watching as a truck hauled away the remnants of their playground. The one thing I've witnessed that feels worse to me is watching children at play during recess and seeing a child, alone in a wheelchair, watching the others from the edge of the playground because the play space is not accessible.

Most of my students say that their favorite day of the entire semester is the first visit they make to the elementary school with whom they are collaborating. Seeing the school and the community, and interacting with the kids, brings the project to life for them and drives home the fact that what they are doing has the potential to have a real impact. That day is always the hardest day of the semester for me. It is the day that I make a promise —unspoken, but nonetheless a promise—that the group of children in this particular school or location will have a new playground at some point in the future. It would be completely irresponsible to walk into the school, get the kids excited about a new playground, ask them to dream big, to teach us something about their world of play, and then not to deliver. In this way, the children at the schools with whom we work are my constant motivation.

The sincerity of the children, their unbounded energy, irrepressible enthusiasm, and their right to have access to safe, fun play is what drives my passion to complete these playgrounds. The children are the sparks that start the entire playground design process and help to keep it going. Once I looked the children in my community full in the face, as individuals and as a group, I found that it was truly impossible to ignore their need for equal access to playgrounds, and more broadly, to anything else.

School Staff: The Galvanizers

If kids are the sparks in the playground design process, the school staff and administration are the galvanizers. My experience with elementary school principals and assistant principals has been amazing. I am convinced that if we want to solve any serious societal issue, we should pull together school administrators, provide them with a summary of the issue, and get out of their way while they plan and execute the solution. Principals get it done with efficiency and with flair. My experience with teachers has been equally inspiring; generally, teachers offer their hearts to their pupils in addition to their brains. Given the fast-paced nature of teaching children and the endeavor to make each classroom a place in which individual students progress at their individual speed and with learning strategies geared specifically toward each student, whenever I visit a school, I am awed by the commitment of educators. Compared to K–12 teachers and administrators, I know that I have the easy job.

School staff members offer sage advice to my students as they work on their playground designs. They will tell the students how they see it with as much bluntness as the children who talk about play. Here is a small sample of the marching orders that school administrators and teachers have given to my students with regard to playgrounds:

1. This area of Baton Rouge has the highest rate of crime, the highest AIDS rate, the highest school dropout rate, the lowest educational level, and the least amount of parental involvement. And yet our school is a high-ranking school. We are nowhere near failing. Make our playground as good as our school is.

2. We are the best school in the world, and everything you've heard about us is true. We want the best playground to match the best school.

3. I want you to keep these things in mind when you are designing a playground with our students:

- The mobility of the students is super high (some are homeless).
- There are some students with really good home lives and some students with really rough home lives.
- Our aim is to make all students as comfortable as possible at our school.
- I'm concerned about the social and emotional development of my students; there is very little social interaction at school because kids don't have a good environment, like a good playground, in which to build social skills and to have social interactions. We need a playground in which we can teach students to share, to be nice, to talk things out, a place that opens up the soul of our students.
- We will find business partners to make this project happen. I'm good at begging.

4. At this school, we try to instill a sense of competition and pride. We want our students not only to do things in life, but also to develop their helping and giving side. The playground will be a real jewel for this community. There are beautiful homes on the other side of the street, but our kids are on this side of the street, without a playground. They need to know that the community cares about them. I would like to say thank you on behalf of myself, my staff, and the children at the school. If this playground comes to fruition, I'll be the one snotting and crying that day.

5. We want our new playground to be so good that when people are driving down Route 1, they'll see it, pull over to the side of the road to get a better look, and think to themselves, "Wow, I want to send my kids to that school!"

6. As you can see, my pre-kindergarten students have nothing to play on except three little tree stumps. The kids love their tree stumps and do a lot more with those tree stumps than I would ever imagine, but really, they're only three little tree stumps, for twenty-five children at once. Anything that you do will be an improvement on this playground.

My students get really excited when they speak with the children about the playgrounds because these conversations fire my students' imaginations. The conversations that my students have with school staff make them sit up straight, take notice, and start using their imaginations to generate concrete playground design concepts. School staff members encourage my students get their houses in order, so to speak.

Sometimes my students are challenged by disagreements that may take place among teachers. For example:

Teacher one: "There will be no swings on this playground. I have scraped screaming children off the grass more times than I can count, and I will not have another of my children hurt."

Teacher two: "The most developmentally important piece of equipment on a playground is a swing set. We need swings. They are my number one request."

Teacher one: "Swings are dangerous! There are plenty of other activities we can add to the new playground without adding swings."

Probably the most common conflict occurs over benches. Many times, principals say no to benches because they do not want any place on the playground where teachers can sit during recess. The principals typically want their teachers to be up and about during recess, actively engaging and supervising the children. The first request from teachers is frequently benches. When asked why, they will often say that they really need a place to sit and rest during recess, since they're working nonstop in the classroom.

School staff are caring, dedicated, and have strong opinions about their children and their schools. Although staff members might disagree about some things, they are united in their care for students and their commitment to education.

College Students: The Facilitators

In the context of playground design, I work with college students closely, more closely than anyone else in the process. My students are adults, but they are young enough adults to be able to solidly connect with the children with whom they collaborate. My students' days on a playground are less than a decade away, whereas I'm more like 3.5 decades removed.

College students are facilitators in the playground design process. They are placed into groups and must learn about playground safety standards and engineering design in short order. They take all the information that the child play experts share with them, the marching orders from school staff, the community history, and the hopes and dreams of the community, and they weave it all together to form playground design concepts. During this process, they have to contend with each other. Sometimes students will have difficulty agreeing on all or part of a design concept. They may have conflicts based on personality; for example, some students may approach their work in a leisurely manner while others approach their work promptly. Some students tend to act decisively while others tend to consider all the options. Finally, some students are uncomfortable with solving an open-ended problem or trying to find middle ground when community partners have different perspectives. There is not a single, correct solution to a playground design; while there are correct ways to complete the design, there are many possible solutions. This situation is one with which many college students have had limited experience. When student groups come to the first iteration (draft) of their design concepts, after being reviewed by other students in the class and by me, the concepts are evaluated by other stakeholders in the process.

Sometimes, my students have to develop a thick skin to appreciate fully the importance of critique in the process. When my students present their initial design concepts to the children, they might hear comments like this:

- We hate this playground idea!
- That game thing is ugly!
- Can you move the swing further away? We like to play chase in that area.
- Yes, we changed our minds completely from five weeks ago. We used to want the wavy slide, but we all decided that we'd rather have a slide where you can race each other instead.
- Where's my whale?

Student designs are also evaluated by the school staff, who usually put the children in the driver's seat as far as choosing the actual equipment on the playground, but who drill the students on playground safety and force them to justify everything they've proposed, which sometimes leads to major changes in the playground design. For example, the school staff knows where temporary buildings may be constructed in the future, and we never want to put play equipment on the site of a new building, whether permanent or temporary. The staff also provides design input on things like proximity of the proposed equipment to the major exits of the school, drinking fountains, and bathrooms, as well as the spatial splits between children in different grades.

Student groups incorporate all changes and suggestions into the second iteration of their design, which they present in a detailed report, and which results in the students completing the course. This is the end of the line for the vast majority of my students, but not for a few enterprising souls. If a student displays a flair for and understanding of working with the community, I ask them to be part of my playground research and design team. These students work with the community to consolidate additional ideas and the numerous student design concepts into an ultimate, complete playground design. These students also work with me to write proposals to fund the playgrounds and write bid specifications to describe in detail the proposed design to the company that will either install it or will supervise the volunteers who install it. Finally, they, and about a third of their classmates, volunteer to help build the playground that they had a hand in designing.

I have students who are repeat offenders, who so enjoyed participating in a community playground design build that they sign up for every build thereafter. Initially, the volunteer playground builds included the school community (teachers, administrators, parents, members of the community) and my biological engineering students. After a while, biological engineering students invited their friends, and so did the school communities. The result has been a burgeoning volunteer pool. Whereas before we might have had to advertise to get enough volunteers to build a playground in a timely manner, we now have to limit volunteers because so many sign up, from all corners of Louisiana.

The college freshmen to whom I teach playground design compel me with their personalities, energy, and attitude; they are committed, engaged, and interesting. All are bursting with potential and are poised for success; most are terrified of failure. I believe that part of my job as a professor, besides teaching students how to think and how to create playground designs in conjunction with community, is to take every single student on his or her terms and to be a transducer—something that amplifies energy and changes its form—on their behalf. My students are already on an upward trajectory; I do everything possible to grab them and push them skyward, so that they can change their potential energy into kinetic energy, to make their dreams become reality. I don't try to change the students' fear of failure; instead, I encourage students to act in the face of fear instead of being paralyzed by it.

I vividly remember being a college freshman. It was the most dangerous time in my life, because I felt like I knew a lot when I really knew very little. I was lucky to fall into the right crowd (a bunch of study nerds) and, with the help of my family, was also lucky to have built a strong enough sense of self for when I hit resistance as a college student. I went for help from an instructor in an engineering graphics class, who told me that it had been scientifically proven that men had superior spatial abilities, and he wasn't sure why I was in his office or what he could help me with, because it was clear that I didn't get it and didn't really belong in engineering in the first place. It is active resistance, like this incident in my graphics class, and passive resistance, like being on your own for the first time and trying to fit into a new environment, that makes first-year students vulnerable.

I've heard other professors (luckily, very few) declare that they can tell if a student "is cut out for" engineering based on the student's performance in the professor's class. I don't believe that, not only because of my experiences as a student, but also because I've seen that arrogant logic break down too many times. I've had students in my freshman design class struggling with algebra who go on to graduate and have successful engineering careers. Likewise, I've seen students enter my classroom armed with high school GPAs above 4.0 and composite ACT scores of 33 and higher who flunk out of LSU. There's a lot more going on in everyone's lives than what happens in the classroom. The first year of college is a critical time: students can fall one way, into complete success, or another, into a world of challenge. It is an honor for me to share a small part of this critical year in the life of my students.

The core of my teaching philosophy is to provide my students with roots and wings. What's awesome is that my students provide me with roots and wings as well, whether they mean to or not. They also provide me with endless energy, which I can draw from at any time because they so freely share it with me. There is something special about being in the presence of lives that are still unscripted but already moored in an interest to serve and to reach the highest ideals of the human spirit. My students are absolutely, no holds barred, fantastic.

Community Members and Other Players in the Process: The Catalysts

On an initial look, it may seem that once you get the sparks (children), the galvanizers (school staff), and the facilitators (students) together, their collective input would be enough to complete a playground project. In practice, it just isn't so. You may have all the ingredients to make the cake, but without the oven, all you have is cake batter. The community members and other players in the process are the metaphoric oven, the catalysts. They provide the means and energy to complete any playground project. Here are the catalysts:

The fire plugs. Every playground project has at least one fire plug, a person whose passion is focused on moving the project toward completion. Sometimes it's a principal, assistant principal, or dean of students, sometimes it's a teacher, sometimes it's a concerned parent or the president of the Parent Teacher Organization or School Improvement Team. Fire plugs are a critical part of the process because they are positioned to provide everything you might need on the ground. Talking to a fire plug is like drinking from a fire hose; generally, fire plugs are effusive and energizing. They do first and talk second. Sometimes, they do both simultaneously.

The ladies. Any community lucky enough to have a group known as "the ladies" knows their value and respects their wisdom. The ladies have graced almost every single school project with which I have been affiliated. They are typically matriarchal elders of the local community who have had a long-lasting, positive influence on the community's members. The ladies possess revered recipes, which, when crafted by their experienced hands, result in food to die for; schools are usually in charge of providing meals for volunteers during community builds, and they often ask the ladies to take charge of this portion of the process. The volunteers who give the best of their hands and hearts in building the playground have their stomachs nurtured with the best food on the planet during lunch, and their souls nurtured by the understated pearls of wisdom that the ladies dispense alongside the food. If you ever find yourself down and out, just find a group of the ladies and hang out with them for a couple of hours. You will find yourself calm and inspired and focused on the things that count. My yoga teacher, Carmen Board, will say of some yoga poses, "You feel happy in your head, happy in your heart, and happy in your belly." Hanging out with the ladies is just like that.

Community foot soldiers. This group takes a unique form every time we work with a different community. It is the trusty group of people to whom the fire plugs turn to get things done. People who act as community foot soldiers include parents of children at the school, members of the Parent Teacher Organization or School Improvement Team, members of community and/or service organizations affiliated with the school, members of local organizations with a service mission, and members of local universities. Community foot soldiers do anything from volunteering to build the playground to helping fundraise to directing traffic on build days, and just about anything in between. This group is critical because its sheer size makes the job easier. It would be a Herculean effort for a handful of people to build a playground, but fifty to one hundred people toiling together makes short work of any playground build. Community foot soldiers are wonderful because they don't ask for anything except marching orders.

Funders. Playgrounds are an expensive undertaking. You have to pay for the equipment (and the freight to have it shipped to your location), site preparation, installation (it is cheaper to pay someone to supervise a volunteer installation than to pay for the playground to be installed professionally), and installation materials, such as concrete and tools. Most of these materials are common, but you need lots of sets of tools, which can break or sprout legs like pens do when they magically leave offices forever. When that's all done, you need to put playground safety surfacing under and around your play equipment; sometimes you need to build a containment area to keep the surfacing in place. By the time you add everything up, playgrounds can have a pretty hefty price tag.

We have built small phases of a playground for as little as $6,000 (years ago) and big playgrounds for approximately $100,000 (though I've only been treated to a budget this big three times). I like to estimate that the average playground costs about $50,000. More than half the time, though, we don't get this much to build. We can usually do some damage with $20,000 to $25,000. This is a lot of money to ask a community to generate. Some organizations will give big chunks of money, while others chip in a little just once or a little at a time, over time; individuals also give large and small donations. Funders are a key part of the process because without them, our good intentions would remain only in our hearts and minds.

Angels. Paul Loeb, the high-profile activist who has written *Soul of a Citizen* and other books on community, has talked about how people get intimidated about serving the community because the only community activists with whom they are familiar are Martin Luther King Jr. and Rosa Parks. Most people who observe the incredible accomplishments of these two extraordinary people think that there is no way that their actions would ever compete, so they get discouraged about doing anything in the first place. Loeb coined the term "everyday heroes" to remind us that you don't need to aspire to incredible heights in terms of service in order to make a significant impact.

Joe Howell, who you met in Chapter 1, is an everyday hero in Baton Rouge. Unless you are affiliated with public schools in East Baton Rouge Parish, you have probably never heard of Joe. He is quiet, soft-spoken, and blends into any crowd. He is many things to many people, but to me, he is the playground angel. He works as hard anyone I've ever met and displays incredible integrity. Joe is an angel because he volunteers at all our playground builds and encourages his employees to do the same; because he patiently answers every question my students ask; because every single principal in the parish has his number on speed dial; and because he never stops working on playgrounds, even though playgrounds are not specifically part of his job description. An angel is not a prerequisite to success, but it sure helps to have one.

The successful orchestration of all these members of the community—the sparks, galvanizers, facilitators, and catalysts—reminds me of the old folk story about stone soup. This is the story of several travelers who come upon a village; the travelers have no food and no money, and no one in the village (which is also short on food) offers to assist them. The travelers do have a pot, however. To it they add water and a large stone, and they place the pot over a cauldron. The villagers are curious and ask the travelers about what they are doing. The travelers reply that they are making a very tasty stone soup, but that it lacks a little flavor; might anyone have spices to add to make it taste better? The villagers go to their respective homes, and each returns with just a little spice, potato, carrot, and the like to add to the soup. The result was a feast that was shared by all.

The input of all the people on a community-based playground design project is like creating a tasty stone soup. Everyone gives a little of something—ideas, inspiration, information, food, money, good will, or playground safety surfacing. When everyone adds their contribution to the pot, we wind up with a playground that will serve the entire community for approximately twenty years. Here are two examples of stone soup in the context of playgrounds.

We undertook a project with University Terrace Elementary School to enhance its playground. We were under a time crunch because the playground build was also serving as a community project for a service-learning conference. University Terrace has a dedicated staff and principal, and it also has a devoted community partner base, including members of the University United Methodist Church and members of the East Baton Rouge Master Gardeners Association. University Terrace formed an executive steering committee that was comprised of school staff, the community partner groups, and LSU students. The steering committee split into several active subcommittees, including fundraising, volunteer building, safety, and food. Almost every subcommittee had one community member and one LSU student as co-chairs. The subcommittees worked diligently for five months leading up to the community playground build. The project culminated with a $45,000 budget, 47 community partners, and over 150 playground volunteers from 3 countries and 14 states. Volunteers installed new play equipment, a greenhouse, and an herb garden in a one-day build.

Brusly Elementary approached me with a dream and a purpose: to overhaul their fifteen-year-old playground. A fire plug of the first order, assistant principal Sheila Goins, set out to raise funds for a new playground at her school, with the school community, especially the kids, focusing on designing it. Sheila got the entire community excited. The town council donated trees to the playground. Local businesses such as Burger King gave a percentage of profits every Friday for weeks to the playground fund, and members of the Brusly community duly ate at Burger King every Friday as a result. Sheila approached a member of the New Orleans Saints and persuaded him to donate football tickets and signed Saints memorabilia to the school; she then organized a raffle with the donated items as prizes, raising almost $20,000. She organized a school play day that featured school teachers and administrators kissing a pig for the playground, recorded the event, and submitted the recording as part of a proposal to KaBOOM! for outstanding play day. KaBOOM! is a national nonprofit organization dedicated to building playgrounds throughout the United States.

Brusly made the finals of the KaBOOM! contest and was then dependent upon the community to vote daily for their play day; five play days were featured from all over the country, and the top two vote-getters over a one-month period would each receive a $10,000 grant. The entire Brusly community voted, as did LSU Community Playground Project supporters and members of the broader community. Sheila appeared several times on television to encourage the entire Baton Rouge area to vote. Brusly came in second place, averaging about 2,500 votes per day; voters hailed from several nations and 23 different states. The ensuing community playground build featured almost 250 volunteers, many of whom had voted daily in the KaBOOM! contest, and who worked together during a two-day build to install the $47,700 playground. Members of the New Orleans Saints came to dedicate the playground after it was completed. For me, the highlight of the dedication was seeing Tracy Porter sprinting in a high-step style reminiscent of his "pic-6" in Super Bowl XLIV, with more than one hundred squealing children running in his wake.

Collectively, the people who have shared their time and talents with the LSU Community Playground Project are my inspiration. People are truly the key to everything. They remind me in so many ways and in so many capacities that we can and do accomplish extraordinary things when we do ordinary things together.

While we try to teach our children all about life,
our children teach us what life is all about.

—*Angela Schwindt*

Playgrounds Rule and Playground Rules

Everyone knows the basic rules of playgrounds, which go something like, "Wait your turn, listen to your adult caregiver, and don't bully anyone." There are of course more detailed rules, and plenty of important information about playground safety that many adults should and don't know. Some of this information is common sense, but much of it is not. If you are interested in learning more about becoming an advocate for playground safety, please consult Appendix 1.

The set of playground rules in this chapter are those that I have formed while working with local communities and the wonderful people who reside in them on our quest to design and build playgrounds.

1. You Can't Do It Alone

When a local community collaborates with the LSU Community Playground Project, we need the hard work and input of about five hundred people on average. Our teams are big enough that we can still function without one person, even one who is a major player in the process.

I could not design and build a playground by myself. I have only one mind, one heart, and one set of hands. Adding many others into the mix ensures an abundance of brain power and ideas, a diversity of perspectives that is critical to making the playground a place that speaks to everyone and addresses the interests of the varied constituencies who will use it, and a collective will to complete the job. The last item is particularly useful when considering the many and varied targeted tasks that make up the entire process. Some people might want to work on securing funding, while others might have a passion to participate in the building. I am always especially thankful to the ladies who pour their hearts into providing food and nurturance for tired, dusty playground building volunteers.

The best thing about *you can't do it alone* is that the cumulative, collective total of everyone's actions is bigger than each individual's actions added together. Scientists and engineers talk a lot about synergism, which means that the whole is greater than the sum of its parts. In math, it would be something like $1 + 1 = 3$. It's the idea that by adding things together, something magical happens in which you get even more productivity or output than you'd predict by just adding things together ($1 + 1 = 2$).

There has been great synergism in every playground project in which we have participated. Sometimes it's easy to see synergism in action—for example, watching a playground come into creation during a 6.5 hour build day because two hundred volunteers are simultaneously working to construct it. The nonprofit organization KaBOOM!, which builds playgrounds all over the United States, has mastered the art of the 6.5 hour build, and we've collaborated with them on three playgrounds.

At other times, synergism is a little more subtle but just as powerful. For example, when a fourth-grader named DJ proudly gave my students a tour through his school playground, there was synergism in the way that his confidence swelled the more he spoke, and the way that the resolve of my students snapped into place as a result like electricity running through a transformer. There is something absolutely synergistic about the process of transforming hopes and dreams from ideas into physical form. I find that everything I give to the playground project comes back to me in even bigger ways; such synergism would never happen if I worked alone. We accomplish extraordinary things when we do ordinary things together. Every playground we've built is a testament to this concept.

2. Once It's Yours, It's Yours

You might think that if the community design process ultimately results in a playground with a predicted lifespan of at least twenty years, provided that the playground maintenance plan is well executed, you wouldn't need to revisit the design for about twenty years. It doesn't work like that. *Once it's yours, it's yours* means that if we have worked with a school once and they come back because their needs have shifted and changed, we will put them at the top of our list and work with them again.

Villa del Rey, the second school we worked with, is a playground that we designed and built in two phases, based on when we could scrape the money together. We used about $10,000 to build half of the playground in the spring of 2001 (phase I) and then used $9,000 to complete the playground construction six months later (phase II).

We were in the pioneer days of the cell phone in 2001, when cell phone towers were not exactly a well-established part of the landscape. Belinda Martinez of Agrestics handled most of the supervision of the Villa del Rey playground construction and had one of the only cell phones on site. She was in frequent communication with Agrestics personnel Kenny (her curmudgeonly uncle) and Robert (her earnest father), both of whom also possessed cell phones. I don't know if it was the cell phone–to–cell phone communications between them that were a challenge or just the cell phones in general, but whenever Belinda was taking or receiving phone calls, she had to climb to the top of a ladder to talk. Belinda spent much of her time on the construction site stationed atop the ladder, and we quickly realized that she was a talented multitasker: she could talk meaningfully on the phone, provide construction supervision with verbal and nonverbal cues through a crude but clear form of construction sign language, and balance ten feet off the ground, all at the same time.

We worked as hard on this construction as we had on the Beechwood playground, but everything went a little more efficiently because this time a number of volunteers were experienced with the playground construction process. We rented a Bobcat to dig all our holes, and there was no red concrete anywhere. Phases I and II each took about four days to finish.

When completed, the new Villa del Rey playground was red, white, and blue, attesting to the school's patriotic spirit. It was proudly situated at the front of the school and served kindergarten through second-graders. There were approximately three hundred children at Villa del Rey in 2001; the third- through fifth-graders had a playground at the back of the school that was old but serviceable, and the principal was happy with the status of both playgrounds. She called me a few months after the playground was done to say that the kids loved it and the neighborhood did too, not only because she had opened the school playground to the kids in the neighborhood, but also because some of the neighbors had confided in her that they felt that their property values had increased because of the new equipment and the welcoming atmosphere it created. Everyone was happy, and I thought to myself, "Case closed" on Villa del Rey.

Seven years later, the principal of Villa del Rey called back. The school's population had almost doubled since 2001 due to two factors: normal population increase and an influx of survivors from Hurricanes Katrina and Rita. "T-buildings" (temporary buildings) had been erected on the back of the school grounds to handle the onslaught of students. The T-buildings had eventually encroached upon, and then overtaken, the playground for the third- to fifth-graders. The equipment on this playground had just been torn out, and the kids were left with nothing but an open field much smaller than that to which they were accustomed. The principal asked if we could return to complete a phase III design for the third- to fifth-graders.

The same week that Villa del Rey called, I made a routine visit to the school district superintendent's office to discuss system-wide progress on playgrounds. During that meeting, I was handed a stack of letters written to the superintendent by the third- through fifth-grade students at Villa del Rey regarding the destruction of their playground. "FEMA stole my playground!" one letter declared. The student's interpretation was understandable, and the frustration expressed in every letter was heartbreaking. The superintendent's office wanted to know if we could assist Villa del Rey with a new playground.

These heartfelt requests made it easy to say yes. My playground design team immediately began collaborating with the students, teachers, and principal (who was different from the principal in 2001) to develop a design.

The school raised $7,500 through a cookie dough sale organized by the teachers but executed by the students—my college students sold some cookie dough as well and added about $500 to the budget. My students then wrote a successful $1,000 grant proposal to the Case Foundation for the project. Our $9,000 phase III playground budget in 2008 didn't go nearly as far as the $9,000 phase II playground budget we'd had in 2001. We picked out four pieces of equipment, including a challenging climber and a swing set, and those four pieces of equipment took our entire budget. Playground angel Joe Howell saved the day when he provided surfacing for the equipment. Upon getting approval from his employer, he also executed the actual installation of the equipment with three of his fellow employees.

During the seven years that had elapsed between the completion of the K–2 playground and the grades 3–5 playground, a lot had changed at Villa del Rey. Our financially lean phase III effort worked well because everyone —especially the entrepreneurial Villa del Rey students—took ownership to ensure that all the kids at the school, whether playing in the front or the back of the school, were effectively served.

Once it's yours, it's yours means that if the community partner's needs change over time in regard to the artifact you've collaboratively created, you are committed to ensuring its continuing success over the long haul (both the artifact and the collaborative relationship). Sometimes, *once it's yours, it's yours* means that you stay on the road with your community partner even if that road takes you places that you never thought you'd go.

In the spring of 2007, one of the sections of my playground design class was collaborating with South Boulevard Elementary School to develop a new playground to replace the existing equipment, most of which was forty-seven years old. Halfway through the semester, when nine student groups were collaborating with the kids at South Boulevard to develop playground designs, we got word that the school was going to close during the next year. All the kids were being sent to a nearby school that was being renovated and getting a new playground in the process. It was the first time that anything like this had ever happened, so we dutifully completed the South Boulevard designs on paper, but stopped the process when the semester ended.

Three years later, I was contacted by a group of parents at South Boulevard and was asked to support them with designing a new playground for the school. The group did not know that I had collaborated with the school's children, teachers, and principal before. I was horrified because I thought that the school had been closed for two years, but the parents informed me that they believed so much in the French and Spanish immersion program featured at the school that they had banded together back in 2007, educated the school board about their program and their plight, and managed to keep the school open.

With this news, I contacted the parish school system, which indicated that South Boulevard was going to close two years in the future. The dedicated parents were not convinced that the school would close, though they acknowledged that due to downtown development and a lack of space at the historical school building, there was a good chance that the school would be moving. So, they wanted to know, could we design a moveable playground? The answer was yes, definitely.

At this juncture, the group of parents jumped into the same high gear I sometimes witness in children playing together on a playground on a perfect spring day. They ran a fundraising campaign and used the non-profit status of the Parent Teacher Organization to retain full control of their $20,000 budget. They worked with me and Joe to identify equipment, vendors, surfacing, and a good location on the school grounds on which to install the equipment. They even interviewed vendors about the warranty for their equipment and the environmental sustainability of each company's equipment manufacturing process. The parents got South Boulevard student input on which equipment to order, placed their order, and dedicated their professionally installed playground just eight months after contacting us. The school negotiated with Joe to pick up and move the equipment if necessary, and the parents have set aside funds expressly for this purpose.

When I work with a school community, I make a commitment to that community for the long haul. When we design a playground to last for twenty years, we hope that the design will effectively serve the community for its anticipated lifetime. Sometimes, circumstances can change so drastically that the initial design or solution isn't suitable for the new situation—whether it's new kids, more kids, a new location, or something else entirely—and so we have to change our solution to keep up. Part of this principle is having integrity in the community design process and a commitment to serving our community partner faithfully over the long haul.

Another part of this principle is making sure our presence in the community is consistent so that people always know that we're approachable and willing to serve. The phase III Villa del Rey request came from two channels simultaneously—from the school's principal and from the superintendent's office—because we were visible and had regular communication lines established. I didn't realize that South Boulevard Elementary School hadn't closed down, and the parents didn't realize that I'd worked with the school three years earlier, but despite these factors, the parents knew that there was a group at LSU who collaborated with public schools on playground design, so they found us and asked. For my part, I promised myself to pay better attention in terms of following up on the fate of school closures, because theoretical closings and actual closings are two different things.

Service-learning guru Janet Eyler said of community-based work, "Complexity is not a problem, it's a feature." *Once it's yours, it's yours* is a rule that honors this complexity while addressing it at the same time.

3. Little Victories Can Have Big Impacts

Sometimes working on an issue can seem so overwhelming that you might think your actions amount to nothing and that no appreciable change will occur. In practice, I have found this not to be the case. I am always amazed at how making small changes, in the grand scheme of things, can have big payoffs.

The first time my class and I visited a local school, for example, the principal told us that currently there was no recess at the school. This was news to me, and my students were dismayed. They thought, "Why bother to design a playground for the children at this school when no time is built into the day for them to play on it?" The principal said that the kids played on their existing playground before and after school, but that there wasn't enough equipment to handle all the kids at recess during the school day, and the resulting behavior issues weren't worth the trouble of having recess. Nonetheless, we faithfully kept on with the design process. Based on the principal's comments, my students focused on trying to get the biggest bang for the buck with equipment so the elementary school students would have plenty of activities to choose from on the playground. After this playground was built, the principal immediately started having recess for the students. No behavioral issues surfaced. We have had similar impacts with recess being expanded after school playgrounds were upgraded.

Early on, we realized the huge impact that penny drives have on playgrounds. The children who share with us their dream playgrounds feel a kinship to the new playground at their school because they have had some say in the playground's creation. This kinship turns to ownership if the kids have put any money whatsoever into helping to build the playground. We saw this concept in action for the first time with the children at Villa Del Rey; their penny drive provided $800 of the total $19,000 budget for their new playground in 2001. Those kids owned the entire play space. I even heard a young child proudly proclaim, "I bought that!" when pointing at the new playground. Since then, many schools have organized penny drives to engage the children in the funding portion of the project. The penny drive at University Terrace was the most diverse, with coins donated from approximately ten different countries.

I have mixed feelings about penny drives. On the one hand, I don't think it's fair to ask a child to pay for a new playground; on the other hand, if putting in five pennies makes that child feel like they own the place, perhaps a penny drive is okay. Playgrounds built using penny-drive funds tend to be taken care of and maintained really well; children don't trash or vandalize what they value and worked together to buy.

If you look at the overall budget of a playground and the percentage of the budget that comes from a penny drive, you might think the impact of a penny drive is small. Although it may be minor from a sheer dollars-and-cents perspective, the impact is huge when the children in a community take ownership of their playground and, more broadly, their surroundings.

Sometimes little victories occur when you're not expecting them, as with penny drives. Other times, little victories occur because you fight for them. After Hurricanes Katrina and Rita, many community groups worked together to try to improve the quality of life for survivors of the hurricanes who had evacuated to the Baton Rouge area. A number of local community organizations whose missions involved advocating for children grouped together to form the YK Coalition. YK had a double meaning; it stood for "Youth of Katrina" and also meant "Why Katrina?" I first worked with this group, as well as the Baton Rouge Rotary Club, on playgrounds in Renaissance Village.

Renaissance Village was the largest trailer-park city ever established in the United States. It was located in Baker, Louisiana, about ten miles north of Baton Rouge, and was home to approximately 1,600 people (including more than 600 children) when its population was at its zenith, approximately one year after Hurricane Katrina.

Some community groups focused their efforts on Renaissance Village and began working with the Federal Emergency Management Agency (FEMA), who was in charge of it, to make life more enjoyable for its residents. The groups hit a roadblock when trying to construct playgrounds in its grounds. FEMA's position was that Renaissance Village was a temporary community and that the construction of playgrounds would encourage people to stay.

Renaissance Village was hastily constructed on a cow pasture to accommodate hurricane survivors; it contained nothing but trailers and a small mail stop. It had a tall, barbed-wire fence around its perimeter and a single entrance with a police checkpoint. Anyone who spent a minute inside the spartan, guarded grounds would understand the absurdity of the statement released by FEMA, which was focused on the "temporary" side of the temporary community equation.

The community groups, who were focused on the "community" side of the equation, used flexible thinking and problem-solving strategies, working with Harold Rideau, the mayor of Baker, to identify an area of the Baker town square that was set aside for the Renaissance Playground. The area was about a mile from Renaissance Village, and transportation was arranged so the residents could easily access it. Community groups, led by first-year Rotarian and community fire plug Robelynn Abadie, focused their efforts on the Baker town square while continuing negotiations with FEMA to build a playground inside the Village. Ultimately, both efforts paid off. Eighty-two of my students volunteered April 28–30, 2006, to construct the Renaissance Playground, which stands to this day as a memorial playground for survivors of the hurricanes and for the community of Baker, who welcomed the evacuees with open arms.

And FEMA finally allowed the construction of community support services inside Renaissance Village, which were funded mostly by the Rosie O'Donnell Foundation and for which a number of community groups—especially the YK Coalition, led by Charlotte Provenza, and the Baton Rouge Recreation and Parks Department—did grassroots organization and execution. In October 2006, a dedication ceremony was held inside Renaissance Village for three playgrounds (we designed one of them), an adult education center, a water park, and an early childcare center. In this particular case, the small victories achieved through groups working and negotiating together resulted in huge impacts in terms of having something instead of nothing. For people who lost everything or much of what they had, having something instead of nothing was monumentally important.

I have often been asked if I ever tire of designing playgrounds, and my answer is always an emphatic no. This is partially because every community is unique and so its community playground will always be different. This is partly because I am always inspired by the people with whom I collaborate, the children (sparks), school staff (galvanizers), students (facilitators), and catalysts, who collectively provide an endless supply of energy, hard work, and good will. I also never get tired of designing playgrounds because I am always learning something new. The next three playground rules are what keep the design process fresh, joyful, and interesting.

4. Assume as Little as Possible

Making assumptions is such an everyday part of life that it is easy to forget that we make them routinely. These assumptions can be innocuous—for example, choosing a particular route of travel because you assume it will be faster than another. But sometimes our assumptions can be harmful, like the professor who assumes that they can determine if a student is cut out for engineering based on the student's performance in that professor's class.

Engineers are professional assumption makers. That's a big part of what we do while designing something. The first step in engineering design is defining the problem to be solved or the artifact to be designed. There are many assumptions in this part of the process—for example, who will use the artifact, who will benefit from it, how it will be used, and so on. Assumptions enable engineers to quantify a problem and to use engineering methods to solve it and/or to create an artifact to address a need quickly and efficiently.

Although assumptions are a routine part of everyday life and a key feature of the engineering profession, I've decided that the best course of action, personally and professionally, is to assume as little as possible. The following three anecdotes illustrate why.

First, the principal of an elementary school was leading a tour of her school's playground for me and my students. There were two playgrounds at the school, one for lower grades (K–2) and one for upper grades (3–5). The upper-grades playground had a basketball court, a grassy area, and an area where kids could sit at a picnic table. The principal explained that she always kept her girls and boys separated during play, and that she rotated each group weekly between the basketball court and the picnic table, with the grassy area in between serving as a buffer zone. She explained that the girls and boys were always separated because the girls beat up the boys— and she meant it. Many of my students laughed, but the principal was not kidding; behavior issues on playgrounds are no small issue, and most principals will go to great lengths to address them.

Admittedly, it was the first (and to this day remains the only) time I'd ever heard a principal talk about girls beating up boys. I usually hear a different reason for gender separation in upper-grade playgrounds, which is that boys and girls are beginning to discover each other in a romantic sense and schools want to minimize the chances of this happening. But the issues that each school faces with its playground and its pupils are specific to the school. If we had assumed that girls and boys were separated because of potential attraction rather than violence, we might have included features in the playground design that didn't address the specific issue that the school was facing. Creating the wrong or suboptimal design by making assumptions is something I try very hard to avoid.

Second, I was privileged to witness the tearing down of a wall of mistrust between some of my students, a wall that had been built with assumptions. During the Villa del Rey build, there was one student volunteer who a group of my high-achieving students felt was a party boy with little substance. This student—I'll call him Jeff—was fun-loving and gregarious, and he did not commit the substantial time or effort to his studies that the other students did. Normally, my students aren't overly concerned about the academic commitment of their peers, but since most classes in biological engineering involve the planning and execution of group projects, my high-achievers were sometimes frustrated with the way that Jeff's social calendar took precedence over his commitment to completing his portion of group projects.

As the playground construction process got underway, the high-achieving students quickly noticed that Jeff was very familiar with a construction site, more so than they were. He taught them the ins and outs of using a post hole digger and running a wheelbarrow. He quickly became the students' gold standard with respect to his combination of strength, endurance, work ethic, and knowledge of construction. Try as the students might, the only area in which they could approach Jeff's input was work ethic.

For these students, Jeff morphed from "the party boy with little substance" to "the committed student with towering strength" during the construction process. Toward the end of our week-long, phase I construction, Jeff dyed his hair purple. While I can't say for sure, it is my belief that the high achievers would have rolled their eyes and muttered "party boy" all over again if they hadn't just spent a week on the construction site with him. Instead, they said, "Cool hair, Jeff," and kept working.

Jeff and my high-achieving students volunteered on both phases of the playground build, and during phase II, Jeff was "one of us" in the students' eyes. It's not that Jeff suddenly developed an ironclad study ethic; he did not. It's that the high-achieving students realized that there was a whole lot more to Jeff than his interest in what fun-loving Cajuns call "passing a good time." With the playground project, I have been lucky to witness the ways in which playground structures are built while assumptions are destroyed.

Finally, during the years in which I've been collaborating with communities to design playgrounds, I've experienced several defining moments, interactions that I will never forget. One occurred in Florida, where I was watching my little half-sister play in a softball game. Alicia, another player on my sister's team, was deaf. During the game, my father was bragging in the stands about the LSU Community Playground Project, and he mentioned that our latest partnership was with the Louisiana School for the Deaf. Apparently Alicia's mother overhead this conversation, because after the game she approached me with Alicia in tow. The little girl, whose gravity-defying braids, quick smile, and spunky personality were reminiscent of Pippi Longstocking, used sign language to explain to me that she couldn't play on most playground slides because they were made of plastic. Alicia wanted to know if I could design a playground that included slides she could use. Her mother explained that Alicia used cochlear implants, which include electrodes surgically implanted into the ear canal to improve hearing. The static electricity buildup that can occur when playing on plastic slides can blow out the electrodes in a cochlear implant, which could potentially require surgery to repair.

I had never heard anything remotely like this about playground equipment. When I returned home, my students and I charged into the literature to more fully research what Alicia and her mother had told me. We learned that cochlear implants are in fact susceptible to electrode blowout. Surgery is almost never required to repair the implants, but kids have to go to an audiologist to get the implant recalibrated if they experience static electricity buildup on the playground that exceeds the rating of the device. Cochlear implants can be turned off to avoid electrode damage, but then the kids have to play in silence. Other playground construction materials, such as metal, do not create static electricity buildup because such materials can be grounded.

Our design choices for the Louisiana School for the Deaf were either to use plastic slides and make sure that the children had their devices turned off before playing, or to use metal slides and have them not think about it. We left this decision up to the community partner, who ultimately chose plastic slides, combining this choice with a commitment to educating students about turning off their implants before going onto the playground. The phenomenon of cochlear implants causing static electricity buildup on plastic is one I never would have considered. The way in which it was brought to my attention by Alicia, who signed slowly for me so that I could understand her dilemma, is something I will never forget.

In each of these cases, making routine assumptions could have led us down the wrong path. When the principal was discussing why she separated her students by gender, I realized I was learning about a behavior issue I hadn't heard about before and that contradicted most of what I had observed in schools to that point. It made me remind myself not to assume that I understood the behavior of all third- to fifth-grade children based on my previous experience. Similarly, my students realized that there was a lot more to Jeff than they assumed. The danger in assumptions like the one my students made initially is that we don't take full advantage of the assets each person brings to a project if we judge or marginalize them.

In collaborating with the Louisiana School for the Deaf, I learned that there are sometimes factors in a situation with which I might be completely unfamiliar. Had it not been expressly communicated to me, I would have assumed that all play equipment was fine for children with cochlear implants and I would not have known to warn the children who use these devices and their caregivers about the potential dangers in using plastic slides. This playground collaboration made me realize how critical it is to research situations to ensure that the things you're ignorant of are out in the open. And you still need to be careful, because even then, you probably don't know everything!

I realize that making assumptions is a normal part of living and in some cases is necessary for quick, efficient problem solving. But experience has shown me to make as few assumptions as humanly possible, to choose those assumptions very carefully, and constantly to question them to make sure that they're appropriate and correct.

5. Listen with Your Heart and Your Ears

Throughout my community playground design experience, I have learned that listening is an art. To do it well, you have to listen not only with your ears, but also with your heart. Listening, really listening, is a challenge, because the human brain can process about 500 words a minute, while the average person can speak about 220 words a minute. It is easy to let the "unused" portion of your brain, the part that could handle another 280 words per minute, wander. I like to tell my students that's why they can look at me while I'm talking with seemingly complete sincerity and interest while thinking about weekend plans at the same time.

In order to listen to another person properly, I consciously put away all distractions, drive all other thoughts out of my mind, look the person in the eye, and concentrate 100 percent of my mental energy on what they're saying. I know I don't listen properly enough. When I do, I have come to realize that I am not just listening with my ears. When I listen, really listen hard, other parts of a situation will speak to me, sometimes in frequencies picked up by my ear canal and other times in frequencies picked up by my soul.

For example, I recently worked with Twin Oaks Elementary School on a playground for kids enrolled in pre-kindergarten and kindergarten. The designated play area had sparse equipment, and the most interesting piece was a small gate that was positioned hundreds of feet away from everything else. It was painted red and was such an interesting artifact that my students and I immediately began calling it the "gate to nowhere," because that is what it was, literally.

On a later visit, we learned the story about the gate to nowhere from Principal Christa Bordelon. Originally, the gate was the entry to a playground that was so old it had been removed for safety issues. For some reason, however, the gate was not removed. Christa then told us that her predecessor had made great use of the gate in the following way: during recess, she'd bring the pre-kindergarten and kindergarten students out to the playground and line them up in front of the gate. She'd ask them where they wanted to go, anywhere in the universe. When the first child in line had thought of a suitable place, she told that child to run through the portal—not through the gate, but the portal—and to yell where they were going as they did so. This activity was one of the kids' favorites.

After listening to Christa's story, I realized that what we had labeled the "gate to nowhere" had actually served as the kids' "portal to anywhere." If I had listened with only my ears, I would have heard the story of why the gate was still there. If I had listened and thought about it, I would have realized that I made an incorrect assumption (this was not a gate to nowhere, but a piece of equipment that was still being used). I listened with my ears, and I thought about it, but I also listened with my heart, which told me that Twin Oaks was a school that made something big out of something small, and used the kids' imaginations to do it. In my heart, I realized that the portal to anywhere was reflective of the soul of the Twin Oaks community, whose teachers and principal were determined to elevate the experiences, imaginations, and dreams of their children despite a lack of resources. The school was sending a message to its students: you matter. You can do anything.

You can go anywhere. I heard all of that, loud and clear. Joe and Christa and the school system secured a $100,000 grant from the Lowe's Charitable and Educational Foundation to fund the Twin Oaks playground, and with it, we added lots of really cool playground equipment. But in deference to the children's love of the portal and as a testament to the school's soul, we left the gate. The portal to anywhere is still a part of the Twin Oaks playground.

Listening is not always easy because the act of true listening requires a lot of effort. Listening can present further challenges because acting on what you hear with your ears and your heart can be complex and some-time contradictory. When my students visit with elementary school students to start brainstorming playground design concepts, they tend to organize the things they hear from elementary school students into two categories: things they can address (swings, slides, monkey bars, climbers, seesaws, merry-go-rounds) and things they can't (pools, lions, spaceships that will fly to Mars and back during a twenty-minute recess). My students frequently ask me how they're going to design a fifty-foot-high tree house with a slide coming out of it that leads to a pool with a whale in it, or a roller coaster, or a horse-drawn carriage that kids can ride around the playground, or a place where the kids' family dogs can romp with them. I explain to my students that it's important for them to listen to everything and to not throw out the ideas they can't design in a literal sense. How we translate the collec-tive brainstorms, dreams, and imaginative ideas of children into features of a playground is the art of engineering design. My students have to listen to, digest, and try to capture the spirit of everything they hear in the play-ground design.

My students are also sometimes frustrated when they hear things that contradict each other. For example, kids might really want monkey bars, but a principal might say something like "Absolutely no monkey bars. I had a set taken out last year after three kids broke their wrists in three months. After that, I haven't had any bone breaks and I don't want to add equipment that will cause them. I want my babies to be safe." Or teachers might request benches as their top priority, and the principal will say, "I do not want any benches on my playground. If they are there, my teachers will sit on them during recess, and I want those teachers on their feet, interacting with the kids." Trying to figure out how to accommodate contradicting requests is another art in terms of engineering design. We depend a lot on our community partners for guidance, and we have to listen carefully to get to the crux of these competing desires.

Another complexity in terms of listening is listening to what is not said. Take the nonverbal message given to the pre-kindergarten and kindergarten children at Twin Oaks. Their school playground for sixty students had less play equipment than the single-family dwelling whose chain-link fence separated the two properties. The Twin Oaks children had the portal to anywhere, a small geodesic dome climber, and a bucket ball, while the children on the other side of the chain-link fence had swings, a tree house, a rock wall, and a slide. It felt particularly sweet to finish this playground, which provided a better nonverbal message for the elementary students. Ultimately, it had three different kinds of slides, overhead fun wheels, swings, and a balance beam.

Sometimes what is not said is, "I don't trust you enough to tell you the story of my community." Listening with your ears and also with your heart enables nonverbal messages like these to permeate, so you can take the time and make the effort to build bridges over things that tend to divide us, such as unflattering assumptions and judgments.

Parkview Elementary School is adjacent to a large cemetery, and a four-foot-high chain-link fence separates the cemetery from the playground. The principal told us, "We keep the children inside and have no recess when funerals are near the fence line that runs along the edge of our playground. This is because some of my kids will go to the fence and offer condolences to the funeral goers. Others will ask mourners, 'Is he really dead and can I see him?' My students dance and sing to bagpipe music when there's a funeral with Scottish rites. They also 'hit the deck' whenever there's a 21-gun salute, and because of this, kids have gotten hurt when they're on the basketball court."

After my initial thoughts, which ran something like, "Who zoned this?" (that is, which came first, the school or the cemetery?) and "How is it that kids in one area of town would assume fireworks or a blown transformer when they hear a 21-gun salute, while others would take cover?" I started thinking about what to do with this issue.

What nonverbal messages do we send kids when they grow up playing next to a cemetery? What are we saying if we erect a green barrier between the playground and the cemetery? Are we covering up death? One of my students said, "We should leave the fence as is and let the kids play next to the cemetery. Kids should grow up knowing about their own mortality." My first instinct was to disagree, but this particular student was an Iraq war veteran with a unique perspective; two weeks after uttering this statement, he withdrew from my class to return to serve our country.

Though we have not completed this playground, we have planned to erect a green barrier between the school and the playground when we obtain funding for the new playground. Still, the questions raised by the Parkview playground haunt me to this day. Short of moving the school (which is not an option at this point), there are no easy answers. No matter what, there are nonverbal messages for the students at Parkview.

6. Watch for Unintended Consequences

The second law of thermodynamics can be stated in many ways; one way is that the universe (or a part of the universe) tends toward greater disorder. Newton's third law of motion says that every action has an equal and opposite reaction. These two laws form the basis of much engineering problem-solving; in terms of community design, they present themselves as unintended consequences. Sometimes the universe acts or responds in ways that you didn't expect or predict; sometimes equal and opposite reactions are not immediately obvious and may show up generations down the road. Sometimes unintended consequences can be humorous, sometimes minor, but sometimes they can be stunning or devastating (and sometimes both at the same time). Here are several examples of unintended consequences from my playground travels:

The Beechwood bench. My students painstakingly selected and designed areas for passive play on the Beechwood playground, and teachers used one of those places to punish kids who displayed poor behavior during recess. What we intended as a quiet, imaginative platform for play was being used as a way to encourage kids to behave.

Runaway gravel. Because we had a bare-bones budget at Polk Elementary School, we used gravel as a playground safety surfacing material when we collaborated to upgrade the school playground. Although the gravel adhered to playground safety recommendations, after several months the principal begged to have the surfacing replaced. The surfaced play area was close to an asphalt basketball court, and when kids left the play area, they inadvertently took gravel with them in their clothes. Because of this transport factor, gravel found its way onto the basketball court and caused several kids to slip and hurt themselves while playing basketball. The slipping is something that one could have seen coming, as well as something that could be controlled with good maintenance. What we didn't see coming was this: three of the school's vacuum cleaners had been ruined because kids inadvertently tracked in pieces of gravel on their clothes, and janitors vacuuming classrooms had experienced gravel lodging in their vacuum cleaners and breaking the suction pumps. LSU alumnus Shaquille O'Neal and LSU student athletes held a day of service for renovating the Polk Elementary playground, and they replaced the surfacing with engineered wood fiber, which doesn't transport as easily as gravel does, which doesn't cause blacktop wipe-outs during basketball, and which doesn't break vacuum cleaners.

The Cutie Patootie Center. I was hired as a consultant to design a playground for kids six months to three years of age inside Renaissance Village, a playground that was later named the Cutie Patootie Center. My task was to design the inside of the play area only; a company had been tasked with designing the raised concrete platform underneath it (the entire area was designed to be removable, since the Village was a temporary community), the shade structures within it, and the fence that surrounded it. The reputable company followed standard protocol by using the fire code to design the fence surrounding the playground, with 4" wide openings between the fence slats. But the 4" wide openings were head entrapments. A head entrapment is generally an opening on a playground between 3.5" and 9", in which kids—particularly preschool age and younger—can get their heads stuck. Head entrapments are potentially fatal, and the kids who are susceptible to head entrapments are little ones—in this case, exactly who the playground was designed for. I contacted the organization that hired me, they contacted the company, and the fence was replaced with 3" openings, which were not head entrapments.

Playground laws. As a certified playground safety inspector, I am a strong advocate for playground safety. But the enforcement of proper playground safety recommendations can have unintended consequences. Some states have enacted strict laws for playground safety, and in so doing, they set the bar so high that very few playgrounds could ever reach recommended safety levels due to expense, a very short time frame for coming into compliance, or both. The consequences for not being in compliance were so severe that many playground operators in those states removed their playgrounds entirely. The unintended consequence was that in trying to make playgrounds safe for children, the law served to deny kids access to them. Although I am an advocate for playground safety, I am also an advocate for policies that make sense, and in this case, I believe that a combination of mandating standards for playground safety within a reasonable time frame and with appropriate resources (or ways for playground operators to secure those resources) is the way to go.

I have numerous memories of the playgrounds I frequented as a child. I remember teaching a neighborhood child to swing, and I remember how proud I felt when he finally got the rhythm of leaning his body and pumping his legs, and the way his effort sent him skyrocketing. I remember climbing what seemed like vast monkey bar structures and hanging upside down on them very carefully so that I wouldn't fall headfirst to the asphalt below.

I once tied my brother to a playground post at dusk with a full moon looming in the sky, told him that the hound of the Baskervilles was coming to eat him (we watched Sherlock Holmes on TV as children), and went to my family's apartment half a block away to eat a popsicle. When my mother started calling for him from the front door a few minutes later, I snuck out the back, untied him, and brought him home. He didn't tell on me, but I got my just desserts several months later when he dared me to see if what he'd heard at school was really true, that your tongue would stick to a metal pole in the cold. The same pole that I tied my brother to on a pleasant summer evening became the one I was stuck to on a crisp winter day. Rather than waiting for him to bring me warm water to help unstick my tongue (which he ran to get, because at the core, my brother is a sensitive, merciful soul), I pulled hard and left a dime-sized chunk of skin on the pole.

I remember playing "Stay" on a merry-go-round, when I and five other children wrapped ourselves around the handholds on a merry-go-round while six other children worked together to spin it. The winner of the game was the one who stayed on the merry-go-round the longest. I gritted my teeth and narrowed my eyes to deal with vertigo as centrifugal force snatched my playmates one by one from the merry-go-round. I finally let go seconds after I knew I had won the game, and my momentum hurtled me through the air and straight into a thick wooden wall intended as a playground safety surfacing border. I was knocked out for a few seconds, and when I came to, I accepted my playmates' congratulations before staggering home to my mother.

Growing up on playgrounds taught me how to compete, how to cooperate, how to behave properly and, in the cases when I didn't behave properly, what might happen if I didn't. If I think about my experiences on playgrounds from both sides of my childhood, I believe that the rules in this chapter apply to playgrounds in a literal sense, but they also ring true throughout my life, far beyond the playground:

You can't do it alone.
Once it's yours, it's yours.
Little victories can have big impacts.
Assume as little as possible.
Listen with your heart and your ears.
Watch for unintended consequences.

Adversity is like a strong wind. It tears away from us all but the things that cannot be torn, so that we can see ourselves as we really are.

—Arthur Golden

Triumphing over Murphy's Law on Steroids

The playground collaboration between Howell Park Elementary School and the LSU Community Playground Project tested my mettle like no playground ever has. This project bludgeoned my will, laid bare my lack of patience, and almost broke my heart. As always, the partnership itself was inspiring, but the roadblocks we faced together were formidable.

Howell Park started the way that almost all playground projects do, at Joe Howell's request, based on his list of schools in order of need for new playgrounds and our conversations about these schools. Shortly before the spring semester of 2006, we made the decision that one section of my playground design class would collaborate with Howell Park. Hurricane Katrina had resulted in the influx of one hundred children to Howell Park a few months earlier, and in the wake of these new students, the already small, dilapidated playground had seemed to shrink even further.

My students and the students of Howell Park did a fantastic job on their collective designs. I remember in particular the excitement and eagerness of the kindergartners, who seemed to love their new school and were elated about the possibility of a playground to supplement their 35-year-old climbers, exercise bars, and slide.

My playground team was in the process of creating short videos to show-case designated schools in their quest for a new playground, with the idea that potential funders might be more interested if we could make each project come to life on the screen. The video about Howell Park had none of the lightness of the other two schools we were working with at the time; the mini-movie sounded more like an SOS than a pursuit of a playground, and rightly so. In the wake of Hurricane Katrina, effectively managing all the changes in the Howell Park community was a challenge. Armed with collective will through the Howell Park–LSU collaboration, a video of the project, and a commitment to follow through by Howell Park principal Mary Langlois, we set out on the quest for funding.

I spend much of my time writing proposals to fund playgrounds. There are two basic rules for writing proposals. First, you have to be specific in order to tell the story of a particular school community effectively, by describing the collaboration that produced the playground design, establishing the need for the new playground, and explaining why the playground and the community are worthy of funding. Second, you don't want to write more than one proposal at once for the same playground in case they both succeed. You don't need double funding for a single playground; you need funding for each specific playground. An exception to this rule is if you are writing to ask multiple sources to commit a percentage of the budget.

Howell Park was the eighth playground we designed in collaboration with the community. It was the twenty-third playground we actually completed. During the almost five and a half years it took from the start to the finish of this project—a period longer than World War I—we started and finished fourteen playgrounds. The money for these other projects was sometimes supplied by the schools and through other grants, many of which I authored or coauthored. Sometimes funding can come about in a cruel way. For example, while we had a proposal pending for Howell Park with one organization, a proposal we submitted to a different organization for a different school got funded. This meant that the other school got their money and we moved on to bid specification writing and building, even though Howell Park was ahead in the queue.

Probably my biggest mistake was thinking that the Baton Rouge Area Foundation (BRAF) would look favorably upon a playground proposal. BRAF is an organization that administers the grant process for hundreds of different granting organizations. They do many wonderful things for our community through grant funds, but a playground for Howell Park was not among them. I was working with a BRAF program officer who suggested applying to different funds based on their mission and past funding record. On the basis of the information from the program officer, I submitted the Howell Park proposal to a number of different funds managed by BRAF and was successively turned down by each. The funding officer suggested that I drop the amount I was asking for to be more competitive. As the rejections mounted, I slowly whittled down my request from $50,000 to $25,000 to $15,000. When I was finally told that I should ask for $2,500 after submitting to eight different funds, one after another, I gave up on BRAF.

The ninth proposal I coauthored was one in which I had a lot of confidence because I had been told by the program officer that it was a slam dunk. The agency had money to fund eligible projects, and with the reputation our program had, if we could work within the confines of the proposal, there was a very, very high chance that we'd be funded.

The originating grant agency was the Corporation for National and Community Service, which had granted the University of Louisiana System (of which LSU is not part) funds to support service-learning projects in higher education for universities in that system. I had a connection to Greg Granger, a professor and Director of the School of Social Sciences at Northwestern State University, which was a member of the University of Louisiana system. We endeavored to complete and submit a proposal that would involve Northwestern State students and LSU students working together on an alternative spring break project to build the Howell Park playground. Greg and I spent two solid days working on the proposal, and it was comprehensive and complete. All was well until I hit a wall with my own university that I could not negotiate.

Prospective grantees must follow the stipulations of a proposal request or it won't be funded. In this case, the proposal required that the lead institution get more than 50 percent of the total funds. Northwestern State was the lead institution because it was eligible for the grant funds and because it was administering the alternative spring break for their students to come to Baton Rouge to work with LSU students. The program also required a 1:1 match, meaning that between us, Northwestern State and LSU had to provide at least the same amount of funds that we were asking the granting agency to provide. Matching is not difficult because it is possible to pledge time committed to the project as money, so that your salary (or the percent of it you spend on the project) counts as a match. We asked for $30,000, $20,000 of which was set aside for the playground equipment for Howell Park. The rest of the funds were committed to funding the alternative spring break.

LSU refused to approve this proposal, and approval was required before the proposal could be submitted. When questioned, the Office of Sponsored Programs cited a rule to the effect that LSU was not allowed to provide more matching money than we were getting from a funding agency. It was possible to get a waiver so that an LSU investigator could offer a 150 percent match with respect to the total being granted, but in this particular case, the amount of money that would actually enter LSU, $1,000, was far below our total match to the project, which was in the range of $20,000. It didn't matter that of the $29,000 of funds that would go to Northwestern State, $20,000 would go directly to Howell Park, and therefore to a local project to which LSU was directly linked. It also didn't matter that not a single dollar of the $20,000 we were matching was cold, hard cash—it was time, time that would be committed to the project anyway.

I returned to Northwestern State to see if they could pick up more of the matching funds, but they were already tapped for as much as they could provide. I appealed to LSU to allow this project to be submitted, but was denied. Deeply frustrated, I called Greg to tell him that our two straight days of work was for naught because LSU would not let the proposal be submitted for competition.

The most odious part of the entire process was being told a week later by the Office of Sponsored Programs that in order to clear this proposal from the queue, it had to be withdrawn from LSU's electronic proposal routing system. When I told them to withdraw it, they replied that the only way for this to occur was for me to withdraw the proposal. I asked why I had to be the one to withdraw it, especially since I was not in favor of this course of action. They told me that this was the only option available because they didn't have the ability to withdraw the proposal. I still get angry when I think about clicking that withdrawal button.

At this point, I was riding the biggest dry streak of my career in terms of writing proposals. I had written nine unsuccessful proposals in a row for the Howell Park playground. A proposal for Howell Park had been under review with one organization or another almost continually for eighteen months. During this time, Melissa Wason, one of the students originally enrolled in the class who worked with Howell Park, completed an independent study course with me in which she merged all seven Howell Park designs generated through the Howell Park–LSU collaboration into a single, consolidated design. She also wrote bid specifications for the consolidated design. Principal Mary Langlois had also been writing proposals for the new playground; we commiserated on the difficulty of securing funding for it. The kindergartners who had worked with us on the initial designs were now beginning their school year as second-graders.

My tenth try was a proposal I co-wrote with LSU professor Carol O'Neil to address childhood obesity through a collaboration with a single elementary school (Howell Park), in which we would execute simultaneous programs on nutrition education and on physical education by having kids meet national physical education standards while playing on a playground at the same time. In order for the children at Howell Park to complete the physical education part of the project, they'd need a playground upon which to play. We thus set aside funds to get the playground equipment necessary for meeting national physical education standards. The playground was not the focus of the proposal; the programming for the children was. We submitted this proposal to the United States Department of Agriculture (USDA) on February 1, 2008, and I promptly forgot about it because usually federal proposals are not funded on the first try due to high competitiveness. In June 2008, I was elated when I got word that USDA had funded us. Although it was a back-door approach to getting the playground funded, we now had $21,000 specifically set aside for the playground—the tenth time was the charm!

I immediately called Principal Langlois to share the good news, and it was then that the Howell Park office staff informed me that she was gone. She had done such a great job of increasing high-stakes test scores at Howell Park that she had been shifted to another elementary school in the parish in need of test score improvement. The staff also informed me of a second legacy of Ms. Langlois: one of the proposals she had written for playground funding had been successful. Howell Park had $5,000 at the ready for the new play space, courtesy of Home Depot.

Kandiest Brock had replaced Mary Langlois as the principal of Howell Park. In her office, Principal Brock has a picture of herself with Oprah and another picture of her and her son bundled up in winter clothing and standing on the National Mall on the day that Barack Obama was inaugurated as U.S. president. Ms. Brock's winning personality, quick smile, and go-getter focus on academics made her a natural successor to Ms. Langlois; she was as excited about the new playground as Ms. Langlois had been. I spoke with Ms. Langlois using contact information provided by Ms. Brock and our conversation was a definite high point; despite no longer being at Howell Park, she was thrilled for her old school.

With the proposal-writing dry spell over, I celebrated briefly, informed Melissa (who by this point was a graduate student at the University of Central Florida) of our success, and signed up another student for an independent study project on the Howell Park playground. Because the USDA grant involved executing a physical education playground program called Play On!, we had to revisit the consolidated design to ensure that all one hundred activities of this play curriculum could be performed with it. They could not, so Lekeith Terrell tweaked the design during the spring of 2009, keeping the focus on the creative playground envisioned by the imaginative children of Howell Park, but also adding some equipment to ensure full execution of Play On!. He then rewrote the bid specifications, and in May 2009, we were ready to begin purchasing the play equipment.

While we were trying to secure funding and finalize the playground design, the existing Howell Park playground, which served pre-kindergarten through first-grade students, lost almost all its equipment (the playground serving grades two through five had virtually nothing to begin with). Antiquated climbers and fitness equipment had been removed due to safety concerns; all that remained was a slide and some trees. The memorable kindergarteners who helped to design the Howell Park playground were now finishing the third grade.

Purchasing equipment is usually a straightforward activity; depending on the source of funds, LSU or the school system typically does the purchasing. Over the years, Joe Howell had removed much work from my plate with respect to purchasing; once he and I wrote the bid specifications (bid specs for short), he took them and completed the bid process so that LSU didn't have to. But with a budget split between Howell Park and LSU, there were going to be complications due to purchasing regulations. My department's financial wizard, Donna Elisar, said that the easiest way to handle this process would be to have Howell Park write LSU a check for their $5,000 contribution and then LSU would expend the entire budget at once on the playground. LSU would administer the bid specification process; although this wasn't anything new, the source of funds for the project, federal funds, was unprecedented. To disburse federal funds through a bid process, all state bid laws had to be followed.

Joe and I had been using parish bid law to construct bid specifications for years. In so doing, we had created something of a boilerplate for writing them. Although each playground design is different, we had the same requirements in terms of liability, materials, and installation; writing the bid specs for the various play components wasn't that complicated, so writing bid specs using parish bid law was something that went quickly for us. State bid law is more complicated than parish bid law—much more.

I grew up listening to my father say, "Almost only counts in horseshoes and hand grenades." I like the bid-spec version of horseshoes and hand grenades: careful enough that you get high-quality, durable products but flexible enough that all companies can compete without a focus on minutiae. Parish bid law is like horseshoes and hand grenades—it has all the metrics to make the process fair and just, but not so many to need people trained specifically to handle the details. State bid law is like nanotechnology; utter exactness matters and razor-thin margins count for everything. State bid law is a realm in which I am not trained, and I had to rely on the expertise of LSU budget and purchasing staff member Tiffany Carter to get me through this process.

Like an unwelcome coincidence, the number ten resurfaced, as it took me and Tiffany going back and forth on the bid-spec draft document ten times before it was fully correct. The Howell Park playground bid specification was released for a thirty-day competitive bid in December 2010, but the holidays fell in the middle of this thirty-day period, so the bid was automatically extended to approximately forty days as a result.

When the bid document was approved, I danced with Tony Daigle on top of the table in my department's conference room as the rest of my team laughed along. Tony had joined the team the year before as a graduate student tasked with carrying out all the research on the physical-education portion of the USDA project. He had done a lot of work with me to change the bid specification to comply with state bid law. My team had been listening to the fits and starts of this project in our weekly meetings; somewhere between the sixth and eighth draft of the specs, I had promised them a tabletop celebratory dance when the specs were complete. I remember these couple of dancing minutes vividly. They felt like the first moments of levity on what had seemed like a tortuous road containing twists and turns into difficult territory I had not encountered in all my years of building playgrounds.

Victory was short-lived, however, because prospective vendors started asking questions about what I thought was, and LSU purchasing had deemed, a complete bid specification. According to state (and parish) bid law, if someone asks a germane question about the bid document, you need to provide both the question and your answer to all prospective bidders through an addendum. With bids handled by Joe, if a prospective vendor asked a question that wasn't germane, he'd just tell them so, and that was that. LSU had a completely different policy. If a prospective vendor asked a question, we had to supply an answer, no matter what the question was.

Asking questions is a ploy deliberately used by some vendors to extend the bid period on a project. It buys vendors time while you answer their question(s) and post a bid addendum with the answers; the vendors then get extra time to respond in turn. If enough questions are asked, vendors can effectively get the bid period extended. Some prospective vendors push for these extensions, and I can honestly say I understand why: because the bid process is so complicated, it takes a lot of time to prepare a bid.

I believe in justice and fairness, and I believe in regulation. But I believe in regulation that makes sense. We have created mountains of complexity around regulation, mountains created in response to people who knowingly or unknowingly have cheated the system. I'm 100 percent certain there's got to be a better way of conducting our affairs than to have the vast majority of people who follow the rules suffer the back end of the 80/20 rule, while creative rule breakers continue to forge loopholes that make the mountains increasingly insurmountable.

The Howell Park playground bid had four addenda that collectively answered approximately ten questions; altogether, the bid process was extended one week beyond the allotted forty days. Eight bids came in, ranging from $24,900 to $47,800. As per state bid law, we accepted the lowest bid that met all our requirements and Integrity Recreation got the job. We were ready to proceed to the build portion of the Howell Park playground. Our kindergarten playground designers were now beginning the second half of fifth grade.

From the time that we began the Howell Park playground collaboration to the time that we were ready to order the equipment for the new playground, the sands of the LSU Community Playground Project began to shift under my feet.

In the summer of 2008, Joe and I were standing next to each other holding up a bridge between platforms for a small but adventurous composite structure at Crestworth Elementary School. Volunteers stood some five feet above us, attaching the ends of the bridge to the platforms. We were silently holding the weight of the bridge with four other people when Joe let go. I looked over at him, surprised, because in eight years of working with him, I'd never seen Joe let go of anything. I noticed right away that his face was red and he was sweating, also two things I'd never seen before. I let go of the bridge as well and asked if he was alright. Joe said he needed a drink of water, so we went to the cooler to fetch a couple of bottles and leaned against the Aramark truck bed to drink them. Other volunteers had jumped in to take our places on the bridge. We watched the volunteers working for a minute, and then Joe said, "Damn chemo." His first word was my fourth surprise from Joe in five minutes, because I'd never heard him curse. His second word was a devastation. I couldn't believe it. He told me he'd recently been diagnosed with liver cancer and had just started chemotherapy. Joe finished his bottle of water, stood up, and jumped back into the fray. This instance remains the only time I ever saw Joe slow down, as well as the only time he's spoken about having cancer.

The sands continued to shift, a little at a time. In 2009, Joe told me that part of the company culture of Aramark is promoting people who do good work. He told me that he'd already turned down several promotions and would be able to turn down several more. Eventually, however, he'd be forced to accept a promotion, wherever it was, and it could be anywhere in the country. He assured me that his assistant manager, John Haile, would take his place as manager when and if he got promoted. Joe felt very comfortable with the concept of John eventually being in his place, and so did I. Joe had trained John and all the rest of the people on his staff; John possessed the same work ethic and attitude that Joe did, and shared the same commitment to playgrounds. We all got a lot of mileage out of teasing John for being a Bulldog—a graduate of Mississippi State—which was not hard to miss because John wore a hat trumpeting his alma mater to every playground build.

The economic downturn that plagued the United States starting in 2008 also shifted the sands, in good ways and in challenging ones. All of a sudden, it was noticeably more difficult to get funding for playgrounds. At the same time, having fewer dollars wasn't as much of an issue as it had been in the past because playground manufacturers were hurting for business, and the resulting discounts on equipment components were unprecedented.

A major blow occurred in 2010, when Joe informed me that due to the economy and changes in management, he was no longer allowed to pay for protective playground safety surfacing for our playgrounds. Between 2001 and 2010, based on his original promise to me to purchase surfacing for the playgrounds for which I found funding, he had supplied approximately $110,000 worth of surfacing and building labor (not counting all the weekend hours that Aramark employees have volunteered over the years) to playgrounds at Villa Del Rey, Brookstown, Polk, Cedarcrest Southmoor, Westminster, River Oaks, Crestworth, Jefferson Terrace, and University Terrace Elementary Schools. That windfall was over. Although he could still assign his people to playground jobs—a substantial economic commitment—he could no longer pay for surfacing.

The build phase of Howell Park shaped up with a split budget that was somewhat atypical of the jobs we'd completed before. A further complication was that we had not added money into the budget for surfacing when writing proposals, but we now had to cover that as well. Donna Elisar and I decided to suck it up and pay for the entire $24,900 equipment bill with the USDA grant, even though only $21,000 had been set aside for it. We figured we'd make up the money in a different budget category within the grant, so that the $5,000 grant Howell Park had received could be used to purchase all the playground safety surfacing.

The people in charge of the various parts of the Howell Park playground had several exchanges in the early part of 2011 to organize logistics. Principal Brock was working with Joe to determine the placement of the equipment at the school. Joe was securing bids for the playground safety surfacing. I was in charge of getting volunteers to the site for the two-day installation. In order to schedule those consecutive build days, I had to coordinate with Julie Smith, the president of Integrity Recreation, to have the play components delivered to Howell Park, and with her installer, Scot Givens, to ensure his availability for supervising the volunteers. We set our build dates as March 17 and 18, which didn't interfere with high-stakes testing at Howell Park or midterm week at LSU. With the logistics settled, I put my student team in charge of finding and signing up volunteers. Scot said that he wanted thirty volunteers each day. We asked volunteers to commit a minimum of four hours, either morning or afternoon, and within a couple of weeks we had all our slots filled.

I checked in with everyone about two weeks before the start of the build and immediately heard from everyone except Joe, which was strange, because he always responded quickly to my communications. I called him and left a message but got no response. I was working with another playground almost ready to build at Sharon Hills Elementary, and the principal there told me that Joe was gravely ill and in the hospital. I used my contacts to find John Haile, who told me that Joe had had pneumonia but was home and was going back to work shortly. Not two days later, I had a call back from Joe. He was his usual chipper self and never once mentioned being in the hospital; he just said that he hadn't yet been able to secure the bids for surfacing and was working on it. Joe went after those bids double-time, but it was impossible to get quotes from prospective vendors in time for the build.

Joe and I talked on March 12, a Saturday in which we both were helping to build the Sharon Hills playground KaBOOM! style; we made the difficult decision to postpone the Howell Park build. There's nothing more cruel than installing new playground equipment, putting caution tape around it, and telling the children they can't play on it because there's no surfacing and it's not safe. I let all the volunteers know and told them I'd ask them to sign up again after we established new build dates.

Joe called me several weeks later when all the surfacing bids were in, and I was shocked at the price tag. The lowest bid was $10,700, more than double our $5,000 budget. A lot of the unexpected jump in surfacing costs was the result of fuel charges; the surfacing material was based on a price per cubic yard, but it had to be trucked to our location, and the price of transportation had skyrocketed.

At this point, I launched a fundraiser to try to raise the difference. In order to do so, I had to secure permission from the university, and LSU granted me permission in record time. I sent out a single email appeal to all our playground supporters, and money began flowing in almost immediately.

Joe, Kandiest, and I jumped off a proverbial cliff of faith and reset the build dates for May 6 and 7 based on Scot's availability, which also gave us a little more time to raise the remainder of the surfacing money (and possibly also to get some lower surfacing bids). The timing was terrible for recruiting LSU volunteers, as May 6 was the last day of class for the spring semester and final exams began on the 9th. The major thing driving me to set the date sooner rather than later was that those kindergarten playground designers were going to graduate from Howell Park as fifth-graders on May 24.

The fundraiser was a fun activity for me because it was a little like Christmas every day for a couple of weeks. I had determined that one bag of surfacing would cost $3.05; we needed to raise enough funds to purchase 1,541 bags of surfacing. I also provided a per cubic yard price ($41.25) in case people wanted to give more, but the per-bag idea was based on the thought that college students would be willing to give up one cup of coffee to buy a bag of surfacing. I was wrong about that, pleasantly wrong; the smallest donation we got was for three bags. Students, alumni, service-learning faculty, and members of the community mailed in checks or dropped them off, and some of our most dedicated volunteers gave big. The fundraiser reminded me once again of the power of many who give just a little, but do so together, toward a common cause.

Our Lady of the Lake (OLOL) College shone for us in this capacity; they had taken the playground project scene by storm in 2009, bringing a number of students and faculty to the University Terrace playground build day. After spending a full day spreading surfacing under and around the new play equipment, OLOL College dean of students Phyllis Simpson pledged unilateral support of the playground project. Since then, she has brought a team of faculty and students to every community playground build. Additionally, her students have raised at least $1,000 for the playground project every year since 2009. Through student and faculty donations, OLOL College kicked in $1,523 for the Howell Park surfacing fundraiser.

The fundraising was working, but we were continuing to race time and the build days were drawing ever closer. Ten days before the build was set to begin, Joe returned to his low bidder to see if it would be possible for the company to deliver surfacing while accepting 75 percent of the total payment upfront instead of 100 percent. We were trying to pull together the funds, and we figured that we'd have all the money within thirty days but not within ten. The company informed Joe that their two-week-old bid (bids are usually good for four weeks) had increased by $800 and was increasing every day due to the volatility of fuel prices. Additionally, they said, they still needed 100 percent of the payment upfront. Joe went back to the drawing board on bids for surfacing.

I sent out an email for volunteers about two weeks in advance of the build days. Although the timing was terrible for LSU students, I was not overly concerned about it because the playground project had become so popular locally that we attracted volunteers from all over the city and even from around the state. I usually send multiple emails to recruit volunteers and we usually have to turn away a few people because so many sign up, but for the rescheduling of the Howell Park build date, I only sent one request for volunteers because I was unsure whether the build would actually proceed according to plan or if we would once again be delayed.

The new prospect of delay was due to a fairly new administrator, who wasn't aware of the playground project or the impending build at Howell Park. This administrator was trying to ensure that the playground build—and the completed playground—was appropriate, safe, and successful. He had the best intentions about the project, but he understandably threatened to stop the build until he became aware of every part of it. Joe and Principal Brock spoke with him at length, and I also spoke with him to provide background information on the LSU Community Playground Project. This process placed the playground construction in limbo and I held off on pursuing volunteers because I hated the idea of rescheduling a build twice and turning away our volunteers a second time. The conversations among the administrator, Joe, Kandiest, and other employees in the school system went on through May 5. On Cinco de Mayo 2011, the impending May 6 and 7 playground build was set to proceed at 8:00 a.m., canceled an hour later, set to proceed again at about noon, canceled at 1:30, and set full speed ahead for good at 4:00 that afternoon. Scot came to the Howell Park site on the morning of May 5 to lay out holes for the playground; he was forced to stay on site all day for a job that should have taken one to two hours, until he finally was given the final go-ahead to proceed.

With the build firmly set sixteen hours before construction was to begin, I had essentially no time to pursue additional volunteers beyond my single email from two weeks before. May 6 was a gorgeous sunny day, with low humidity and a nice breeze to offset temperatures in the mid-80s. I had ten volunteers that morning instead of the thirty requested by Scot; additionally, Joe had pledged three Aramark employees for the day.

I began the day with a heavy heart because I felt I had failed to hold up my end of the deal by not bringing enough volunteers to the site. I was also upset because we still had no better bid on playground safety surfacing, so we were not going to install the surfacing at the same time as the equipment, which meant that the kids would see the equipment ready to go but still would not be allowed to play on it. Additionally, the build felt strange because Joe wasn't there to work alongside us, as he had on every build for the past ten years. He had office work to do, and while I understood that (he and I both seemed to having increasing responsibilities that led us into more meetings), it was hard to begin the playground build without his sunny personality, knowledge of construction, and work ethic.

When I was an undergraduate, a professor asked my class to estimate how much power, in terms of horsepower, the biggest, strongest person could deliver. I remember guessing that the biggest, strongest person could provide about one-half horsepower (that is, half the total power of a horse). Others in the class guessed somewhere around the same thing. The professor informed us that in actuality, the biggest, strongest person could deliver only about 0.2 horsepower. Although I believe my professor was correct, I also believe that Joe Howell is a half-horsepower guy. Joe puts 100 percent of his considerable strength into every job he does, but he also puts in his heart and soul. When you add all that together, he contributes half a horse-power to every job. It was strange not to have him out there. Principal Brock was absent too, ill with a bad case of food poisoning. Without the two people I'd worked with most closely throughout the Howell Park job, I felt a little alone on the site.

But I wasn't alone. Three Aramark employees were there, and all three were half-horsepower men, just like Joe. John Heroman, Wayne Knighten, and Willie Thompson have been on so many playground jobs with me that they're as predictable as the rain every summer afternoon in Baton Rouge. I felt buoyed by their presence, as well as by the LSU contingent, (mostly faculty and a couple of brave students) and the group from OLOL College (entirely faculty). We also had several volunteers from the community. Scot was unfazed by the lack of volunteers. He smiled and told me, "Let's just see how far we can get today," and split us into small teams to begin construct-ing equipment.

An hour into the build, Joe called to tell me that he would stop by to say hello later in the day; he also had good news to report. Julie Smith of Integ-rity Recreation had cut costs to the point that she was making no money on the surfacing in order to facilitate the quick completion of the Howell Park playground. He gave me the estimate and I was thrilled; between the drop in price and the money we'd received through the fundraiser, we could afford the bill. I'd have to secure more volunteers to spread the surfacing as soon as it arrived, but we still had a chance to complete the playground before the end of the year, provided that we could get the surfacing delivered in time.

At this point, getting the Howell Park playground finished in time for those kindergarten designers to play on it as graduating fifth-graders had become an absolute must in my mind. I felt the weight of that thought, and the shrinking margin of time to be successful in my goal, like a strong headwind. I was excited about the phone call from Joe, but as I hung up the phone and went back to work, I realized that I was tired—exhausted, in fact.

Phyllis Simpson and I were assembling a bench in the grades two through five play area. The pieces weren't quite fitting together properly, and I was remembering the engineering concept of tolerances, in which you need to specify enough room for two adjacent components to fit together and be easily attached, but not too much room so that the method of attachment doesn't work. That "give" in space is called a tolerance, and I was cursing the manufacturer for erring on the small side of tolerances; our overlapping holes were simply too small to accommodate the bolt that needed to go through both pieces. Phyllis and I were using a drill equipped with a metal cutting bit to increase the size of the holes when we heard someone across the construction site tell everyone to look up.

We did, and we were greeted by the sight of half a dozen Mississippi kites flying in circles above us. Mississippi kites are small hawks that show up in south Louisiana in mid-April and leave in early September. For me, the kites are a harbinger of summer, and their aerial acrobatics are always a welcome addition to the sky. The grounds of Howell Park are large and absolutely beautiful, with a decent number of tall, mature trees; moreover, they are adjacent to the Howell Park golf course, whose large expanse boasts even more large trees. Birds ignore the barriers we erect on the ground to separate ownership and use; for the kites, the Howell Park school grounds and the Howell Park golf course were one and the same: a large, hospitable hawk habitat. My excitement at seeing the half-dozen Mississippi kites became total elation as I watched pairs of kites lift out of the trees in twos, almost like a wedding dance, in which the newly married couple dances, dances in turn with their in-laws, and then everyone else joins the dance floor in celebration. Six kites became ten, became sixteen, and I stood transfixed as I ultimately counted twenty kites jetting through the sky at once, deftly riding the thermals in such a way that I could actually see the air currents.

It was like a moving masterpiece. The kites swooped and called and disrupted the flight of the occasional crow or swift in the air above our heads, and then, two by two, they dropped back into the trees and the sky was clear again.

During that five-minute kite show, something happened to me. I didn't stop being exhausted, but suddenly it didn't matter that I was. I had begun to view the Howell Park playground project as a series of disasters, a job that had long ago lost all lightness and fun; it felt like a chore, like the SOS in that now five-year-old video, and a project I had to endure in order to finish. Those Mississippi kites in the sky that morning were like a beacon to me, a clear signal from the universe that everything was OK and was going to be OK.

I tackled the bench with newfound energy and was treated to Phyllis's description of all the birds in her yard while we continued to fix our tolerance issue. She had just finished telling me that the south Louisiana term for a prothonotary warbler was a yellow swamp canary when Scot came to check on us. He reminded me of one of my favorite engineering slogans: if it doesn't fit, force it, and if it breaks, it needed fixing anyway. With two minutes of Scot's time and his targeted use of a screwdriver and hammer, we were on an efficient path to completing the bench.

As the first day of construction progressed, I was happy to see that the "less is more" philosophy was actually working in our favor with volunteers. Over lunch, Scot told me that he was excited about our rate of progress; already we had completed construction of the swings, track ride, fun wheels, balance beam, and bench. The afternoon would consist of finishing fabrication of the climber, cementing this equipment into the grades two through five play area, and beginning to put together components for the composite structure and spinning equipment in the play area set aside for pre-kindergarten to first-graders.

Phyllis left after lunch, so I joined the decks and poles group for the afternoon and got to brush up on my "pole dance" routine, which involves holding a five-inch diameter, approximately sixteen-foot-tall post in a completely vertical configuration, occasionally picking it up and moving it around in its deep ground hole to properly line up with the deck attachments.

Joe showed up with a big smile on his face, a tie on his uniform, and a pronouncement: he had just accepted a promotion with Aramark. The good news was that he was staying in Baton Rouge; the bad news was that he'd be leaving grounds and maintenance. Joe told me that John Haile would take his place, reminded me that John had the same commitment to playgrounds that he did, and said that he would continue to support our work in any way that he could, especially the playgrounds we currently had in process. "I don't leave loose ends," Joe told me, "so even if I have to work on these playgrounds myself on weekends, they will get done. I promise you." I congratulated him, took a deep breath, and tried to remember the Mississippi kites.

Partway through the afternoon, I stopped to take a water break. I was sitting in the shade against one of the school buildings, reminding myself to remember to drink water more frequently. It's easy to lose track of time on a build, and on sunny, hot days, a person can lose so much moisture through sweat that the next day one can be plagued with a dehydration hangover. Since I was going to be back at the Howell Park build site first thing the next morning, I wanted to avoid that condition.

While I was sitting and contemplating water intake, a little girl walked up to me and said, "You're a girl?" I was struck immediately by the way she asked this question. She knew I was a girl, but something wasn't making sense to her, so she was asking, just to be sure. When I answered yes, she looked at me a moment and asked a second question: "And you're allowed to work with all the boys?" I answered yes again, and told her that lots of girls grow up to work in construction. I then told her a little about building the Howell Park playground. She listened to me, nodded, and walked away without further questions. That one-minute conversation reminded me that our playground builds are egalitarian with respect to gender, and the fact that they are sends a powerful message: there are half-horsepower men in south Louisiana, and there are half-horsepower women, too.

The pre-kindergarten through first-grade play area at Howell Park was situated at the side of the school grounds and was clearly visible to the cars going by on both Winbourne and Brookstown Avenues. While wrapped around one of the composite structure poles during the afternoon traffic rush, I noticed how many cars slowed down, waved, and beeped at us as the orange and black composite structure began to take shape against the sky. People in one car rolled down their windows and yelled, "Looking good!" to all of us. In 2011, Baton Rouge had the seventh-highest murder rate of any city in the country; the highest murder rate within Baton Rouge is in the 70805 ZIP code, the area in which Howell Park is situated. The reverence for children and the support we received from the locals was as steadfast and clearly communicated in the 70805 ZIP code as in the lowest-crime ZIP code in the city.

We had ten volunteers again on Saturday and we made quick work of completing the installation, finishing at 1:00 in the afternoon. Scot was all smiles; he told me that finishing early had made up for all the extra time he'd spent on the site Thursday, when he had to wait for clearance to lay out the holes for the playground. We hugged goodbye, because—like the Aramark guys—I've worked with half-horsepower Scot and his crew on a lot of builds. As I was walking away, he said, "Marybeth, I'm glad you're not egotistical." I turned around, surprised. Although I was glad he thought so and don't think I am egotistical, I wasn't sure what drove his comment.

"Why do you say that?" I asked, and he replied, "I can't imagine calling you anything but Marybeth."

"I can't imagine you calling me anything other than Marybeth either," I responded, "See you at the next build."

Names are interesting things. The first piece of advice given to me by my boss when I began my career at LSU was to go by "Dr. Lima." "Don't take this the wrong way," he said, "but you look young enough to be an undergraduate student yourself. You need to create some distance between you and the students you will teach, and you need to reinforce that you have completed a doctorate. The students need to respect you, and being called Dr. Lima will help to create that respect." So I went by Dr. Lima with my undergraduate students. I told my graduate students that they could call me Marybeth from day one, but almost none of them ever have.

As time has passed, I've come to dislike being called Dr. Lima, not only by my undergraduate students, but by anybody at all. I appreciate the fact that people who call me Dr. Lima do so in an effort to treat me with respect. Elementary school staff and principals are very careful about calling me Dr. Lima; I really wish they'd call me Marybeth (or Ms. Marybeth or Ms. Lima, which fits in perfectly with the culture of southern schools). While I appreciate the respect, the word *doctor* is freighted with formality at least, and divisiveness and pedestal building at most, and I'm comfortable with none of it.

College campuses have great potential to engage with their communities to address critical societal issues, but the ivory gates that surround college campuses are a barrier to engagement. I feel like being called Dr. Lima creates an analogous ivory gate, a barrier that holds others back from engaging with me as a real person. I am not above my community or better than someone who does not have a PhD, just as a university is not above or better than the community in which it resides. We are in the community, an integral part of it. To fully and properly engage with the community, I believe that we need to open up those ivory gates and add our resources to the resource base of our communities, fully addressing community issues as equal partners. I also believe that we need to open up our names and just be who we are, rather than a list of our credentials.

Joe called me on Monday, May 16, to let me know that all the surfacing had been delivered to Howell Park. He said, "You tell me which day you'd like to get volunteers out to the site, and I'll get all my guys out there too, with tools and with the backhoe." I picked Wednesday, May 18, to give prospective volunteers a little time to sign up. I was hoping to have better luck recruiting volunteers than I did with the construction dates, since LSU had finished final exams on the 14th.

At 8:00 on Wednesday morning, I had six volunteers show up in work clothes: Megan Barnum, Tony Daigle, Casey McMann, Brooke Morris, Cas Smith, and Nicole Walker. All were biological engineering students, and all had volunteered previously for at least one (and as many as four) playground builds. Brooke, Cas, and Casey were an angel's hair away from graduating from LSU on May 20, a full four days ahead of the original set of kindergarten playground designers who were set to graduate from Howell Park on May 24.

We had 160 cubic yards of engineered wood fiber to spread on the two play areas. The biological engineers went to work on the grades two through five playground, moving and spreading this material, while four Aramark guys worked around us, building borders around the perimeter of the equipment to contain the surfacing. One other Aramark employee was running the backhoe, which quickened our progress immensely.

The work my students and I did that morning reminded me of the early days of the LSU Community Playground Project, in which primarily my own students worked with me side by side. We had the kinds of conversations that I cherish, conversations that are uninterrupted by meetings or phone calls or emails or fires that need to be put out. We talked about post-graduation plans at Penn State, LSU, and the University of North Carolina at Chapel Hill. We talked about summer plans in Europe, on an organic farm in Ashville, and a vacation to Key West. We talked about demonstrating success in calculus, making sure that summer class schedules were reasonable, and finding new apartments. We talked about our dogs and the entertaining things they do. When I caught Tony alone, I told him very specifically all the reasons why I think he would make a great professor, both because he's considering it and because I know he'd be fantastic at it. To the graduating seniors who were contemplating working in the summer before starting graduate school in the fall, I championed the idea of taking some time off in the summer if they could swing it economically; the last time I took a month off was in the summer of 1989, right before I started graduate school. I told them that responsibilities catch up to you, and if you're privileged enough to have the option to take some time, by all means, take it.

I feel like the king of the tire, from the game that the children of Beechwood Elementary played, back when Beechwood was a vibrant elementary school. I am lucky enough to stand on top of the tire because of the hard work, sacrifice, and support of many people and of the myriad communities to whom I belong, past and present. Thanks to all of them, and to some extent thanks to my own work, today I am privileged to stand exactly where I want to be. As a professor, I believe that my job is to do everything possible to get my students and my community to stand on this tire with me. Students give me many things, but two of the most important are a perpetual supply of energy and a driving desire to succeed in the future. It is partly from the latter that I draw and build on my own passion to live in a just community in which all children have the right, not the privilege, to a safe, fun, accessible playground, as well as a top-notch education. For that, my students are absolutely precious to me. I know that I stand atop the tire on the shoulders of many, and I hope that in turn, my students will stand on mine. Ultimately, our communities and the members in them should all feel like the king of the tire.

At 9:30 a.m. on May 18, my six students and I were talking and shoveling engineered wood fiber with pitchforks, moving it from the giant pile under the swings to the adjacent area where the climber, bench, track ride, balance beam, and fun wheels were located. The Aramark men were making great progress on erecting the borders, and we were on track to complete the entire job in the early afternoon. At 9:35 a.m., we heard a dual B flat, F sharp grinding of gears, smelled a whiff of ozone, and watched in horror as

the giant backhoe sputtered to silence. We all looked at each other, knowing that without the backhoe our relatively easy day had just gotten a whole lot harder. Tony looked at the machine longingly and said, "We just lost our best soldier." The Aramark men ceased building the border to investigate the backhoe. They looked at the engine, conferred for awhile, and planned a course of action: one of the employees went to get tools, another went to buy parts, and the rest went back to border building. John Heroman told me that they were going to fix the backhoe as quickly as possible. "I know how much you need to get this playground finished," he told me, "We'll get it done, probably not today, but tomorrow. I promise."

Brooke Morris was not only a graduating senior, but also a member of my playground design team. Weeks earlier, my six-member team had planned a congratulatory lunch for her on May 18 at one of her favorite restaurants. The non-functioning backhoe ruined these plans. "No problem," said Brooke, when I told her that going across town would result in too much of a work stoppage on surfacing, "Let's just go around the corner for Subway instead. In fact, I'll do the run for everyone's lunch if y'all want to keep working." That's exactly what we did, and we rescheduled the lunch for June.

We continued work all afternoon with a brief stop for lunch and frequent but staggered water breaks to combat dehydration. With the backhoe sidelined, we began using wheelbarrows and tarps to speed the movement of surfacing. I was physically exhausted but lifted at the same time by everyone working with me. There is something very comforting to me about working with the Aramark men. As seasoned veterans of physical labor, they possess the magic combination of joking, talking, and working together that results in great efficiency and progress without the breaking of their backs. They remind me of an army: their service is to the public schools in East Baton Rouge Parish, and they treat this service with as much reverence and respect as a soldier treats her or his country. Working side by side with my students is equally comforting. Although we are not seasoned veterans of labor, we are united in a common task, and while we may not possess the magical combination of the Aramark men, we all know how to work hard.

Despite the grueling work, the day smelled more like victory than defeat. Wayne Knighten's laughter rang across the playground all day long. We all took turns hanging off the top of the swing bar; though it was eleven feet off the ground, the eight-foot-high pile of surfacing underneath it made swinging from the bar a very simple and fun playful break from shoveling and hauling. "We love working with your students," Wayne told me that afternoon. "Love it. We really enjoy their conversation and company. We look forward to these days." Students and Aramark employees slowly took down the mound of surfacing under the swings as we moved it toward the rest of the equipment, while other Aramark workers ministered to the backhoe. With twenty minutes left in the Aramark workday, the backhoe cranked back to life. Every single one of us cheered. Aramark employees called it a day at 2:30, except for John, who stuck around afterward with me and my students to continue the job. At 3:30, he told me that he and his crew would finish the job the next morning, but that if I could bring volunteers again, we'd speed the work along.

I sent out an appeal for volunteers that afternoon, but with only fifteen hours of advance notice, at 7:15 a.m. the next morning, the only two takers were me and Tony. I could stay only until 9:30 because I had meetings for the rest of the day, meetings that I couldn't reschedule. Most of the Aramark men were back at the pre-kindergarten through grade one play area, and so was the backhoe; they were working on spreading surfacing under the rest of the equipment. Tony and I worked on continuing to lower the pile of surfacing under the swings as John hung the swings, which would have been the finishing touch on the grades two through five playground. As soon as he hung the first swing, it was clear that although the packaging was correct, the swing chain length was not; we had swings for an eight-foot frame, not a ten-foot frame. As a result, the swings were about four feet off the ground and not usable.

I left Howell Park as the grades two through five playground, minus the swings, was finished. On my way out, I went to tell Principal Brock that the kids could now use this playground for recess. The surfacing job on the grades two through five playground would have horrified Belinda and Kenny of Agrestics, who taught us painstaking attention to detail and insisted on absolutely level surfacing. The pride Agrestics took in their work was something I believed in strongly and was something I had instilled into generations of playground volunteers as a result. However, time was of the essence and volunteers were few and far between; although the surfacing for Howell Park wasn't an Agrestics-inspired finish, it was a horseshoes and hand grenades job, good enough. The important thing was that sufficient surfacing was under and around all the equipment. And although the children couldn't swing (new swings were promptly ordered and hung over the summer), they could play "King of the Surfacing Pile" underneath the swing frame. As for the rest, John said, "We'll smooth out the surfacing under the swings when we actually hang them. Until then, the kids can compress that surfacing themselves, just by running around and having fun on it."

Tony called me that afternoon to tell me that both playgrounds were finished. He said that he'd been present when the Howell Park students first entered the playground; the fifth-graders (the kindergarten designers) got first dibs on it, which I thought was apropos, all things considered. He also told me that only half the fifth-graders were allowed on the playground because the rest were "on the wall." "What does that mean?" I asked him. "They're in trouble for some reason or another," he answered. I thought that was a shame, but also emblematic of the struggle of the Howell Park playground.

I often encourage my students to try to focus on process, not just outcome. As John Lennon said, "Life is what happens when you're making other plans." The Howell Park playground project forced me to take my own advice, multiple times. Before Howell Park, I had never cried over a playground, not out of unhappiness or sheer exhaustion. This playground took me to that place more than once. I didn't expect to feel elated when the build was finished, and that was good, because I didn't.

A whole lot of process went into the completion of the Howell Park playground: 100 kids from New Orleans joined 400 in Baton Rouge, and of the 500 we initially engaged in the effort for a new playground, only about 100 would be at the school to see it finished; two principals who have raised high-stakes test scores every year in which this project was ongoing; multiple drafts of proposals and bid specifications; 1,948 days from start to finish; bureaucracy at its worst and at its best; a haystack of setbacks; Joe; Julie Smith's company taking no profit on surfacing so we could finish; a committed army of half-horsepower men and women; Mississippi kites.

I think that to an extent, I built a levee of sorts around this entire project, a levee to block every setback or letdown the Howell Park project seemed to attract. If I hadn't built such a wall, I probably would have cried a river that would have added to the record-high flooding that the Mississippi River was experiencing on the day we finally finished the playground. Sometimes you just take your lumps and walk away. It doesn't matter if your head is up or down, the point is that it's still attached.

The kindergartners whose ideas drove the Howell Park playground design had four days to play on their playground as graduating fifth-graders. Four days (actually three days for the half of them who were on the wall) is better than zero days. "Don't feel bad about how long it took us to get this new playground," more than one Howell Park teacher told me, "Remember, those students who are gone have siblings who are here now, and they'll get to use it. Those older kids still benefit too. We all do. Remember that."

While the spirit of neighborliness was important on the frontier because neighbors were so few, it is even more important now because our neighbors are so many.

—Lady Bird Johnson

Community Stone Soup
Breaking the Myth of "Broken" Schools

"How do you define community?"

I was once asked this question in a job interview. I gave a straightforward answer—something along the lines of being united in mutual respect and working together for the common good—but I've thought about the definition of community for a long time and there are a lot of answers to that question. A community can be defined as a group of people who share particular traits (geographical, religious, political, occupational, and so on), a number of groups united around a cause, or all the beings that inhabit a particular environment. While one can pretty easily provide a basic definition of community, my experiences involving community are far more complicated.

The concept of community is at the core of the playground designs produced through the LSU Community Playground Project. Capturing the essence of what makes each school community special, a process I call finding the "soul of the community," is of paramount importance. In my travels through the playgrounds of my community's public schools, I've learned that every school community is different, and that the soul of each specific community is like a snowflake, unique and distinctive.

To be successful in designing a playground that will reflect the unique community it will serve, I encourage my students to figure out the soul of the community and to let that soul be the driving force of their collaborative designs. It is perhaps the most difficult concept that my students struggle with. They'll typically come right out and ask just about every constituent in the process what they think the soul of the community is, getting some wonderful answers in response.

It is difficult to explain to students what it's like when you finally "get" the soul of the community, because when you do, there is no longer any need to ask. The community has stopped being "them" and has become "us." Communities, like schools and like playgrounds, are living, breathing things; you understand the soul of the community when you are part of the living, breathing thing that is the community.

I tell my students that understanding the soul of the community is like hearing your favorite song on the radio. It is the spine-tingling feeling of excitement you get as you hear the initial chord, the bass beat, the lyrics, the refrain, and then that favorite part of your favorite song, the nuanced subtle thing, where you know you've seen and felt through to the heart of the song, its soul. Once my students see through to the soul of the community, that unique ball of people and place and emotions and accomplishments and roots and wings and aspirations, they can begin to translate it into a playground design through activities, art, landscaping, equipment, music, and so on.

The soul of the community is why no playground design we've ever completed is the same. It is also the reason that designing playgrounds is never boring. I begin every playground design collaboration knowing that the soul of the community is there, but also realizing that I don't know it yet. I love to spend time immersed in a school community, listening with my ears and my heart, watching with my eyes and my mind. Inevitably, I come to an understanding of the soul of the community sort of in the way that a painter creates a painting, first with broad strokes, then by filling in detail, and finally through fine tuning. When a painter finishes a masterpiece, that painting vibrates; it puts out energy to those who feel it, an energy that is exciting and calming and uplifting, all at the same time. I feel like I know the soul of the community when I can literally feel it vibrate around me and through me. I get the same calm, happy feeling while in this community that I get when I look at a George Rodrigue or Bill Hemmerling painting. To use my community soul sister Deborah Normand's words, "It's like manna."

The soul of the community is the reason why the portal to anywhere remains at the Twin Oaks playground and why New Orleans Saints cornerback Tracy Porter half-sprinted in high-step style across the Brusly playground during the dedication ceremony with one hundred jubilant children streaming behind him. It's why South Boulevard Elementary has a playground that is ready to move when the school community relocates, and why people executed a "drive-by cheering" on at the corner of Winbourne and Brookstown Avenues as we finished the Howell Park playground.

I have seen through to the soul of more than thirty communities, many of whom are labeled broken, failing, bad, or dangerous. I find them to be none of these things. I see yards as neat as pins and thick, iron bars on windows of houses. I see the faded facades of small businesses surrounded by modern megachurches. I smell potent chemical cocktails that saturate the air and hear the drone of airplane engines. I see live cats and dead dogs, thriving oak trees and peeling paint. I see children who take care of each other. I see groups of people determined to provide children with a strong education and a positive, emotional center in the face of challenges such as poverty and homelessness. I see matriarchs and patriarchs who hope and pray and work for a better life for their children, their neighbors, and themselves. I see struggle and the ravages of economic policy that continues to erode the lives of more than half the population of the United States and beyond. I see grace, hope, and resolve. Most of all, I feel the triumph of the human spirit. I feel it vibrating clear and true and strong.

When my students take the playground design class, they undertake the fairly straightforward process of learning playground safety standards and playground design, the somewhat less straightforward process of learning to communicate with disparate groups of people with different interests and needs, and the difficult process of trying to grasp the soul of the community. The latter involves examining assumptions and learning the difference between serving and helping; it can lead to uncomfortable moments, conversations, and revelations. It is an elusive thing, the soul of the community, partly because you have to find your way within the community, but also because you have to find your way within yourself.

We all make assumptions; they are an everyday part of life, and we tend not to even think about them. As stated in Chapter 3, engineers are professional assumption makers; we learn the nuances of when and how to make assumptions that help to make solving a problem easier and more clear-cut. One of the key parts of the playground design process is learning to make and justify assumptions, while also learning to question and disregard those same assumptions when necessary. I encourage my students to examine every assumption they've got, question why it's there, and whether it's necessary to have.

Some of our design assumptions are uncomplicated. For example, students might ask, "How big is our budget?" Given that we've had money in hand for building our collaborative designs as soon as they're finished exactly twice in about thirty tries, the budget is usually theoretical. I make the assumption that eventually we can come up with $25,000 for any single given playground. Do we assume that if we talk to about 40 percent of all the students in the school, and about half of those students want a spiral slide, that it's a safe assumption to say that the spiral slide is a must on the playground design? Yes, we do, and it is.

Assumptions about people in the school community can be more challenging. In his book *The Tipping Point,* Malcolm Gladwell discusses the concept of a 150-person limit, and how 150 is a magic number of sorts because it is the biggest group of people in which everyone knows everyone else well enough to have close-knit relationships. Many military units, for example, have approximately 150 soldiers; they aren't any bigger because the size of the unit ensures that every soldier in the unit knows every other soldier in the unit. The idea is that every soldier will take care of every member of the platoon, because she or he knows and has a personal connection to everyone.

Our communities tend to be much larger than 150 people. And once you don't know people in your community, it is easy to make assumptions about them, assumptions that in some cases may be less than flattering. Research in psychology has shown that it's easier for people to make decisions that can be directly or indirectly detrimental to other people if the decision-maker doesn't know them.

Most of my students do not know a single person in the school community with whom they are collaborating. Generally, my students are products of the private school system, and many are entering a public school for the first time in their lives. The majority of my students are white; the majority of children in the schools with whom they are collaborating are black. The vast majority of students enrolled in the public school system are poor (approximately 80 percent are on free or reduced lunch). The vast majority of my students are not.

My students are faced with a number of questions, to which they have different answers, and which expose some of their assumptions. Do we assume that everyone has fair access to goods and services in our communities? Do we believe that everyone deserves access to those goods and services? Do we assume that people who are poor are lazy? Do we assume that people who are poor deserve to be poor? Do we assume that people who are part of our communities are decent and deserving, and people who are not part of our defined communities are not? How do we define community?

I try to provide my students with frameworks in which they can start to understand how answering such questions and examining their underlying assumptions will fit into their profession. One easy way to illustrate the social role of engineering is through access—the ways in which an engineer can work to provide people with equal access to goods and services. Playground design is an excellent example because it is strongly influenced by the Americans with Disabilities Act (ADA) of 1990. According to the ADA, a public playground should be accessible to all children, including those in wheelchairs. Students learn what they need to provide to make a playground ADA compliant, which involves providing a wheelchair-accessible route to and on the playground, properly selecting accessible playground safety surfacing, and specifying the correct number and types of accessible play components at ground and elevated levels. If a playground design adheres to these guidelines, as well as those detailed in the Architectural Barriers Act, including the correct dimensions for access, then the playground complies with the ADA.

I explain to my students that in my view, complying with the ADA in this way represents the letter of the law. I then talk about the spirit of the law: how the spirit of the law is that a child in a wheelchair should have access to the entire playground, and that there should be places on the playground that promote play between children in wheelchairs and children who are not in wheelchairs. Providing access is what engineers can do. Certainly, they can analyze and design solutions to problems, but they have to consider those problems in the context of broader issues. If access is a core belief in a democratic society, and I believe that it is, then engineers can and should work tirelessly to provide equal access in the niches in which they work, be they education, health care, infrastructure, food and shelter, environmental sustainability, and so on.

Another concept I tend to drill into my students is the difference between helping and serving. I know that the word *help* has some very specific meanings and some very important uses. In the context of community engagement, however, I really dislike it. As physician and author Rachel Naomi Remen has written, "When you help, you see life as weak. When you fix, you see life as broken. When you serve, you see life as whole. Fixing and helping may be the work of the ego, and service the work of the soul."

I explain to my students that the basis of the playground partnership between university and school communities is shared equality. We are all here to learn. And we are all here to serve. We come together to share our strengths. We do not come together to help each other; we come together to serve each other.

As my students move through the design process and begin to make, break, and critique their assumptions, they may get to a place of greater understanding and also greater confusion. For example, students may understand the issues of playground access and the ADA, but some are left questioning the connection between providing access to a person with a disability (which is entirely justified, because being disabled is "not their fault") and a person who is poor (because maybe being poor is "their fault"). But then my students look at the children with whom they're collaborating at the school, many of whom are poor, and they can't bring themselves to blame the children. It is a difficult place to be.

Difficult places can lead to difficult conversations, which have arisen from initial student comments such as:

"I can't believe that the kids wanted tennis courts. How would they even know what tennis was, living in that neighborhood?"

"What if I've decided that the soul of the community is bad?"

"My heart is broken. I watched this teacher absolutely scream at this little girl today at school. It's like the little girl was a flower and after the teacher was done, she had lost all her petals. The teacher's reaction was totally out of proportion to a simple little question."

"What is wrong with helping?"

Once, while on the way to the partner school in a travel van, a student named "Joshua" was looking out van window when he said, "Where's the watermelon?"

"Amanda," a student seated two rows in front of him, replied, "What did you say?" This question, when stated immediately after something inappropriate is uttered, is usually enough to get a student to think about what he or she said, to adjust accordingly, and to have additional conversation if necessary. However, Joshua completely missed the cue. "I said, 'Where's the watermelon?'" he replied with a smile. Amanda was upset, and when she spoke to him again, Joshua realized it.

"What exactly do you mean by that?" she asked.

"Well, uh, just look around you," he said.

"Yeah, look around you. This is *my* neighborhood, Joshua, and these are *my* people. What are you trying to say about me and my people?"

"I'm sorry," Joshua stammered, "I didn't mean you!"

"Well, who do you mean, then? And what exactly do you mean?" Then there was silence, and a few tense minutes in the van. Joshua had his head down and, uncharacteristically, his mouth shut. When we all piled out of the van at the school site five minutes later, Joshua walked right up to Amanda and looked her straight in the eye.

"Amanda, I apologize," he said, "I was talking without really thinking about it and I was rude. I meant no disrespect to you and none to your people either. I'm sorry." Then he grabbed her in a bear hug.

Joshua's hug was as inappropriate as his initial statements, but Amanda, surprised at first, sighed within his embrace and hugged him back. And after that, they became friends . . . not bosom buddies, but friends.

Difficult conversations can happen at the school as well. For example, take the following account of my student Roger Desanti and his experience as a reading tutor:

> On my first visit to Merrydale Elementary, I went to the class of my reading friend so that we could have our first meeting together. When I called his name, Allen scowled at me; he slunk out of the classroom and when we got outside and began talking about reading, he answered me in single syllables and had his arms crossed and a mean look on his face. When I asked him what was wrong, he said,

"I don't like you."

"Why is that?" I asked. He looked at me and said,

"Because you're white."

I told him that I wanted to visit with him one more time, and if he didn't like me after that, I'd get reassigned as someone else's reading buddy. I asked him what he liked and he gave me some ideas, and before our next visit, I went to the library and picked out four books, all on topics that Allen was interested in. We sat together and read them during our next meeting and at the end of the meeting, Allen told me it was OK for me to continue as his reading friend. By halfway through the semester, whenever I came to class to get him, Allen was not only excited to see me, but called me his buddy and would hug me whenever I came to class to get him.

Generally, my students care, and they care a lot. Some admit to starting class caring only about their grade, but by the end of the semester, the students care about the community with whom they have collaborated. The students have gone through the process of learning about playground safety. They have agonized about what awesome artifacts they had to remove from their dream playground design because that design cost more than $25,000. It's hard to remove equipment from a design when you know that one hundred children specifically asked for it. My students have bonded with the elementary school students through the creative process and through play. They care about the children at the school. They care about the school. They care about the lack of play equipment at the school. They are frustrated about the lack of funding for their school's playground. They tend to leave class asking me, "What happens next?

What indeed? Children have taught us how to play and to be playful, and never to stop being joyful. We have playground designs we've created together and usually have no money to build—at least, not yet. We listen when the teachers, who exhibit a deep commitment to student learning and who have taught us much about courage and resilience, ask for a playground of their own, a placid outside area in which they can regenerate. We listen to the constant, crushing mantra of "Public schools are failing" while we watch principals carry the torch of hope in the face of despair, keep their teachers and students motivated, and model an impeccable work ethic. And we feel the soul of the community, which for me vibrates to the tune of my favorite song, U2's "Where the Streets Have No Name." How do we look at all of this and hold it in our hearts? What do we do about this?

I don't think that there are simple answers to these questions, and even after being involved with community engagement efforts for more than a decade, I'm not sure that I have a full handle on answering them. But here's what I believe we need to do.

Believing in community involves taking ownership. When principals talk about the schools at which they are employed, they use the terms "my school," "my staff," and "my children." Teachers say, "my students," custodial staff and students say, "my school." When principals and teachers talk about the public school system, they say, "us" and "our." Many use the term "my family" in relation to their school. This tribe of people takes ownership and pride in their individual school communities, while recognizing that working together as a coalition is also very important. In other words, they take ownership while not excluding anyone else. Being willing to take ownership of something also brings responsibility for that something with it.

In their search for the soul of the community, my students usually come to the conclusion that on some level, us = them. At that moment and beyond, there is a level of ownership, togetherness, and responsibility that leads my students to the conclusion that community matters, and people matter too. In this way, we all add our individual ingredients to our community's version of stone soup, just as Sheila Goins created community stone soup through the Brusly playground project. When we refuse to engage, and say instead, "it's them," "their problem," "their fault," "their issue, not mine"—when we refuse to bring our marbles to the playground to play—we rob ourselves of an awesome experience and we rob our communities of our contributions. Our stone soup is incomplete.

It's all about assets, not deficits. Every community has assets and every community has deficits. I've noticed that success comes more quickly and easily when we focus on all the assets we bring to the table to address an issue through our collective strengths. We make stone soup with what we have available in our communities, not by aspiring to a recipe that we cannot create until we have all the ingredients, which perhaps we cannot secure easily or at all. We do what we can with what we've got. I've also noticed that once you put everything on the table, so to speak, others are more likely to add their ingredients to the pot.

Blame is like poison. It is easy to blame something from far away. How many times have we heard about the "failure of public schools" and blamed some nameless person or system in response? We blame schools, superintendents, teachers, principals, children, parents. And yet everything I have seen in my travels in public schools points to the opposite. I see people taking ownership and taking responsibility, taking pride and working hard, and doing so consistently under a cloud of criticism and doubt.

I've had numerous principals tell me essentially the same story: "During a community gathering, I heard Person X (a prominent community member) say that public schools are failing.

'Mine's not,' I told Person X. 'I am the principal at [my elementary school]. How would you like to come and take a tour?'

Person X agreed. She came to my school at the appointed time, and I gave her a tour of the grounds. Person X met the teachers, saw the kids' excitement in class, watched students participating in academic and physical education activities, and changed her mind about what was happening at my school. Person X is now a big supporter of my school, contributing to our teacher appreciation fund and participating on the School Improvement Team."

Although it is great that prominent community members are willing to engage with schools and are willing to change their minds as a result of what they observe, it is a slow way to change minds. Schools do not have time to change minds one by one through school tours.

Universities are not immune to blame either. I once watched Saundra Mc-Guire, LSU chemistry professor and national expert on teaching students how to learn, lead a room full of college professors through the following exercise:

McGuire: "Who do you blame when students come to your classroom and they aren't well prepared for learning?"
Professors (amazingly in unison): "High schools."
McGuire: "Who do the high schools blame?
Professors: "Middle schools."
McGuire: "Who do the middle schools blame?"
Professors: "Elementary schools."
McGuire: "Who do elementary schools blame?"
Professors: "Parents."

The exercise stopped there, and even though the message was rhetorical, it bears saying out loud. Blaming parents, elementary schools, middle schools, and high schools doesn't change reality in the college classroom. It is your responsibility as a professor to do whatever is necessary to ensure that your students learn.

In my mind, blaming is a passive activity that wastes time and enables us to feel justified in doing nothing to change or even challenge the basic forces that result in inequity in the first place. Nothing changes if we blame parents—and what do we blame parents for, anyway? With rare exceptions, parents want what's best for their children. Where's the blame in that? Blame does nothing but shift responsibility, typically to nameless, faceless people or entities. It changes nothing. Public schools are not failing our children; by and large, parents aren't either. We are failing our children as a community. Let's take ownership and contribute our assets—our stone soup ingredients—to address the issue instead of blaming someone else.

Think and do simultaneously. Community engagement expert Ken Reardon says, "Generally, we're taught the steps 'ready, aim, fire' in terms of accomplishing something. That approach doesn't work in community engagement. If you do proceed through the steps 'ready' and 'aim' in community engagement, by the time you get to 'fire,' 90 percent of the people you started with are dead, and the other 10 percent are so tired that they don't have the energy left to fire. In community engaged work, you fire first. Fire and figure out where to aim the stream while it's moving, and forget about ready. If you want to get anything done in community engagement, 'fire, aim, ready' is a much better approach."

Be the community fire plug, the everyday hero Paul Loeb talks about. You don't need 100 percent of the knowledge you think you'll need before you start. Thinking and doing are both critical activities. In my experience, thinking tends to be overrated and doing tends to be underrated, and the tendency is to try to learn everything before you start. In order to accomplish something within the community, there is no substitute for doing. Start there. You'll learn along the way.

Part of doing and learning at the same time means that you will deal with situations in which you may feel you don't have all the knowledge you need. I've often wished for more expertise in effectively addressing statements that betray prejudice. Despite my wish, I've found that confronting bias is more an issue of just doing it while being persistent and respectful, rather than being well-versed in critical race theory. The best-case scenario is having all the necessary knowledge before you do something; the reality is that if you wait until you feel like you know everything, you'll delay doing it to the point that nothing ever gets done.

Additionally, when working with community, it is impossible to know everything that you will need to know before you start. Things move and shift and change in ways that you never anticipate, and you have to learn on the fly to address those things to keep moving forward. The only way to move forward is to do and to keep on doing.

Louisiana native Donna Brazile, who got her start in politics at age nine by campaigning for a city council candidate who promised a playground to her community if elected, says, "We're waiting for someone to say, 'The door is open, go through it.' Don't wait for someone to tell you. Find the envelope. Open it. Find the elevator. Push the button. Ride it."

I have been lucky enough to witness and participate in true community engagement. University Terrace Elementary School, which I mentioned in Chapter 2 as a great example of stone soup, is the public elementary school in Baton Rouge where a child will probably go if he or she has come from another country and speaks English as a second language. A number of the students who enroll at this school are coming from countries in the midst of strife, and they and their families may arrive in Baton Rouge with only their lives and the clothes on their backs.

University Terrace has a number of dedicated community partners, including the University United Methodist Church (UUMC), Boys Hope Girls Hope of Baton Rouge, and local master gardeners, who work with children at the school to plant and maintain community gardens. These partners and others provide school uniforms to children in need and office supplies to teachers; many times they provide start-up resources, including furniture and food, to families new to Baton Rouge. The group Volunteers in Public Schools also works with University Terrace to provide Reading and Math Friends, trained tutors who work with children who read and perform math at below grade-level expectations. Approximately fifty Reading and Math Friends work with children at University Terrace at least once a week, and they have made a substantial impact on the academic performance of the children with whom they work.

Among the gardens at the University Terrace are an edible garden, in which children grow their own fruits, vegetables, and herbs, and an international garden, which contains a plant from every country of origin represented at the school, so that every child has a memento at the school that reflects and respects their national heritage. Currently, community partners are collaborating to raise funds to establish a kitchen at the school, where kids can learn to cook recipes using the ingredients they grow in their gardens.

Once each year, University Terrace puts on an event in which plants that have been grown by the children throughout the year are sold to generate funds for future gardening and other related activities, and in which the children give garden tours to the public. I take the student-led tour every year, and every year I wear my sunglasses, because the kids' knowledge of gardening and plants, their pride in what they have taken part in creating, and their inspired narrative moves me to tears every time.

This fabric of togetherness and care at places like University Terrace Elementary School convinces me that community is everything. Communities don't need our help. They need our buy-in. They need our ingredients in stone soup.

I am a proverbial bird nerd; I simply love to watch birds. Having done so for more than a dozen years, I've noticed how much birds have adapted to living around us, especially in urban settings. We tend to walk around and not pay much attention to them, but if we do, we can see high drama going on all the time around us. I love to watch mockingbirds, who enjoy playing games with each other and who amuse themselves by doing aerial somersaults on power lines. Flocks of cedar waxwings blanket the sky of the LSU campus at the beginning of every spring semester. You don't even need to look up to know they're there because their high-pitched song is audible everywhere. If they are congregated in trees, you can hear the collective soft padding of debris hitting the ground as they feed. Ruby-throated hummingbirds migrate through south Louisiana every year at the height of hurricane season. I've watched those hummingbirds navigate hurricane-force winds with ease while the same winds pick up and move hundred-ton chunks of bridge and road. I find birds to be incredible, but they live in "the spaces in between," and tend to be ignored.

I briefly studied chaos theory in a mathematics class in college, and the idea that one can model and predict outcomes in a complex, dynamic system has always fascinated me. Two concepts have become imbedded into my thinking from learning about chaos theory. First, events can be connected in ways that we see and in ways that we can't, but in either case, they are absolutely connected. Second, although we tend to think in concrete dimensions—for example, a two-dimensional drawing or a three-dimensional object—in chaos theory, dimensions aren't necessarily integers. Thus, an object can be partly two-dimensional and partly three-dimensional. An object that doesn't have dimensions that are integers is called a fractal. Such objects often occur in nature (for example, snowflakes). The way I tend to think about "the 2.5 dimension" is as "the spaces in between," the ones not immediately evident to us.

I've had the privilege of working with many communities within the larger one in which I reside. Many of these communities adapt to living around those of us who are "the haves." They are similar to the birds I watch all the time; they live in the spaces in between, where there is incredible beauty and complexity, but where they tend to be ignored by most of us. Just as it's easy to forget that birds are all around us, living their lives around us, it is easy to forget the child who lives a mile away away who may not have access to a safe play space, or food, or safety, or a top-notch education. It is even easier to forget the child who lives halfway around the world and is in the same dire situation.

Each of us is a member of many communities and is defined in part by the community in which we live. In some ways, community all comes down to how we see it and how we define it. And yet chaos theory tells us that no matter how we as individuals choose to define our communities, we are *all* connected. Moreover, we're not only connected to other people; we're connected to all the creatures in our ecosystem and to the environments that sustain us.

How do you see the public school in your local community? Is it the place where supportive learning is occurring or the building that houses children from the "bad side of town"? When the principal of your local public school says, "The children need to know that the community cares about them," do the children know it? How?

I have seen the immense power wielded when we unite around a positive cause and the devastation when we don't. It is my hope that in pursuing a good life for our children, we don't forget about our other children a mile away or four thousand miles away. Children around the world who live in the spaces in between face a metaphorical—and in many cases, actual—gate to nowhere.

I am grateful for the ingenuity of the teachers of Twin Oaks Elementary School, who lined up their students and created the portal to anywhere from a gate to nowhere. To the teachers at Twin Oaks, and to the school staff of the many schools with whom I've had the privilege to work, the children enrolled in our community's public schools are not statistics; they are not doomed to ravages of poverty or inequity. They are living, breathing beings with great potential. They are children who matter, children who can go anywhere and do anything. Just like communities.

Public schools have been called broken. I don't believe that. I believe that our communities are broken. We tend to break because on some level, we've decided that "us" and "them" are so different that our plights are not connected and "they" are not part of our communities. And we need to change our thinking around these breaks. Although we are all different and unique, we are all connected.

Our communities don't have to be broken, with some communities re-siding in the spaces in between. We shouldn't wait for leaders, politicians, or other people to try to address our broken communities. All we need to do is get started. If we can build bridges across our broken places, we can more effectively serve everyone in our communities. You don't need to be an engineer to be a community bridge builder, and you don't have to be an extraordinary person to be a force for the common good. You just have to be a citizen with an interest in service and equality. You have to be willing to stand up and say, "My people, my community, my responsibility."

Metaphorically, we all need to run through the gate to nowhere, to real-ize that it's a portal to anywhere. The children at Twin Oaks are using their imaginations to go anywhere in the world. We can, too. And I hope that rather than going out to Saturn, or going deep into ourselves because of fear of the unknown, that we go home—home to our communities. I'm will-ing to bet that our collective actions and our willingness to add our unique ingredients to our community's stone soup will result in synergistic efforts that will create the best tasting stone soup ever. Everyone who eats it will have bones stronger than titanium, thoughts rooted in fairness and open-ness, and a heart that never succumbs to fear.

One small step for a child, one giant leap for a playspace.

Photo by Nicole Walker.

The ladies of Brusly Elementary School, who cooked delicious meals for approximately 250 volunteers during the playground build. The students at Our Lady of the Lake College enjoyed the food so much that they threatened not to participate in the next playground build unless the ladies did the cooking again.

Photo by Nicole Walker.

Joe Howell and I take a quick break from construction at the Sharon Hills build to pose for the camera. The fact that this playground was about to be finished after more than three years of toiling made us extra happy!

Photo courtesy of Marybeth Lima.

Three of my students take a break from construction at Beechwood to play King of the Tire.

Photo by Marybeth Lima.

The incomparable Kenny, preparing supports for our composite structure during the playground build at Polk Elementary School.

Photo by Marybeth Lima.

Sparks fly as one volunteer cuts excess length from bolts, while two others reinforce the strength of playground support posts.

Photo by Marybeth Lima.

LSU biological engineering students show off thank-you cards created by students enrolled at the Louisiana School for the Deaf during the one-day construction sponsored by KaBOOM! and local businesses on March 25, 2004.

Photo courtesy of Marybeth Lima.

A partial view of the playground at the McMains Children's Developmental Center. Each child at McMains, all employees of McMains, and all playground volunteers were asked to decorate a tile in honor of the new playground. These tiles were then incorporated into a set of benches pictured in the center of this photograph.

Photo courtesy of Janet Ketcham.

Volunteers from Rotary, Kids Around the World, LSU, and the community pose in front of the Renaissance Playground as it nears completion.

Photo courtesy of Robelynn Abadie.

Students at Brusly Elementary enjoy recess.

Photo by Nicole Walker.

Jan Shoemaker standing next to me while I do "the pole dance" at Howell Park Elementary School.

Photo courtesy of Marybeth Lima.

Four human swings enjoy the view atop the Howell Park swing bar.

Photo by Marybeth Lima.

Trying to stay dry during Tropical Storm Faye. Every student in this picture is now an alumnus of Biological Engineering at LSU. Today, they collectively possess fifteen degrees, including one MD and three PhDs. Note Faye the frog, our mascot for the build, below the right side of the roof.

Photo by Marybeth Lima.

Students from Buchanan Elementary enjoy the new school playground.
Photo by Nicole Walker.

Twin Oaks teachers and administrators stand behind the portal to anywhere.
Photo by Nicole Walker.

Although social change cannot come overnight, we must always work as though it were a possibility in the morning.

—Martin Luther King Jr.

A Brief Survival Guide for Community Engagement Marathons

One's perspective changes when engaged in a community pursuit for a long time. My involvement in community has shifted over a period of years as I've worked to integrate my professional and personal interests, but now it is focused with laserlike intensity. Playgrounds are so much a part of my everyday life that they're like signposts in my physical world, where they call out to me when I'm out and about, in my mental world, where I often think about the actions or statements of children at play, and in my spiritual world, in which my need for justice is fulfilled by working to provide equal access to everyone at play.

I have arrived at the following six principles as a result of engaging with my community for an extended period of time. Anyone who endeavors to create change through community work is most likely well familiar with these principles, which are offered in the spirit of marathon journeys that make the world a more fair and just place.

Make Friends with Failure.

Making friends with failure is such an important concept that it's hard to overemphasize. When I talk to my students about failure, I dig out my favorite, "Wake up, this is important" hook, which goes something like this: "According to research, people retain about 10 percent of what they learn in a lecture (which is why I don't lecture a lot). I figure that I'm doing a beyond awesome job if you remember 10 percent of what I say, and I'm thinking that I'm doing pretty well if you remember 1 percent of what I say. Let's assume I'm doing pretty well. If I had control of the 1 percent of what I say that you actually remember, this would be one of the things." And then I tell my students that if they want to succeed in whatever they endeavor to do, they must make friends with failure.

In our culture, we are quick to point to our successes, and we are often just as quick to point out others' failures. Failure tends to be an excuse to gossip about others, a reason to pity others, and a state that everyone would prefer to avoid. Here's the dirty little secret that generally no one likes to talk about: everyone fails. And generally, anyone who is successful also has a history of unsuccessful activities. Dr. Seuss was rejected by twenty-seven publishers before he got a book contract. Henry Ford went out of business five times before launching a successful car company. Marilyn Monroe auditioned for a modeling company and was told she should be a secretary or a housewife. Abraham Lincoln failed as a soldier, a businessman, and a politician before becoming President. Gertrude Stein published her first poem after almost twenty years of rejection. One of Thomas Alva Edison's famous quotes is "Genuis is 1 percent inspiration and 99 percent perspiration." The perspiration involves a lot of failure, and a lot of trial-and-error experimentation.

I have failed many more times than I have succeeded. Sometimes, my initial failure has led to something better down the line. One great example of this is how I got my start in service-learning.

I went to a lecture on the LSU campus by the famous service-learning practitioner Edward Zlotkowski, who was visiting from Massachusetts. After listening to his engaging presentation, I figured out that the method of teaching I was using in my first-year design class had a name and that its name was service-learning. I also learned that LSU had an office of service-learning and that Jan Shoemaker was the director of this office. I connected with Jan. To this day, she has taught me more than anyone about what it means to be an engaged faculty member.

After the Zlotkowski presentation, I did some research and learned that not many engineering educators around the country were teaching engineering using service-learning. I thought that getting the word out about service-learning in engineering was important and would be well received, both because of the "real world" nature of the teaching method, which engineering educators value, and because of the reflective components of service-learning. Since engineers have to be reflective in their problem-solving approaches, I thought that presenting a systematic method for teaching students to be reflective would be appealing to those who teach engineering.

I submitted an abstract about service-learning in engineering to the American Society for Engineering Education (ASEE) conference and my abstract was accepted into the poster division of the conference. Being put into the poster session was a failure; organizers put all the abstracts that are rejected from presentation divisions into the poster session, which gives the poster presenter an excuse to come to the meeting, stand in front of their poster, and hope that those interested in their topic actually show up to talk about it. Attendance at the poster session was typically so poor that conference organizers supplied free wine and cheese to entice people to show up.

I created my poster, went to the conference, and stood dutifully in front of my poster during the appointed two-hour time slot. I had exactly one visitor. Toward the end of the session, Edmund Tsang read my poster, introduced himself to me, and we had a conversation about the service-learning classes we each taught in engineering. He then said, "I am so glad that you're here. The American Association of Higher Education is producing a book series on service-learning in the disciplines. I am the editor of the engineering volume. You are one of only five presenters of the more than one thousand at this conference who are talking about service-learning. Would you be willing to contribute a chapter about your service-learning program to the book?" I was honored and interested, and I agreed to write a book chapter about my service-learning class.

If I had let my failure to present my service-learning work in a regular division of the ASEE conference stop me, I would not have gone to the conference with a poster on my project, I would not have met Edmund, and I would not have published a chapter in his book. The chapter I wrote was my first major publication on service-learning in engineering, and it put my name on the map as a person doing service-learning in engineering. Ultimately, my failure led to a success.

More often than not, my failures have led to even more failures. The Howell Park Elementary playground project seemed like a high-tide failure, with wave after wave of setbacks throughout its five-and-a-half years. The nine consecutive rejections of proposals for this playground were the highlight of failure in this process, but it seemed that failure was a constant companion, from funding to writing bid specifications to securing a playground manufacturing company to unexpected costs and broken installation equipment.

Failure feels uncomfortable. The most uncomfortable part of failure for me is the idea that every failure I encounter during a playground project delays access to a safe, fun play space for the approximately five hundred children who have already delivered their expertise to the playground design and are waiting for the actual playground. The knowledge of these delays grinds into my heart and feels like a weight on my shoulders. And yet, despite the uncomfortable nature of failure, I have learned it delivers much more concrete knowledge than it does uncomfortable feelings. If I am open to its other aspects, failure is actually a fantastic teacher.

For one thing, failure provides me with a discrete data point, which I can use to improve for my next attempt. When researchers like me write proposals to national funding agencies—such as the National Science Foundation, the United States Department of Agriculture, or the National Institutes of

Health—the overall funding rate is approximately 10 percent. This means that nine out of ten applications fail to get funding. Along with their rejection notice, however, each researcher receives detailed reviews of their proposed project, which provide information about how to improve it, should the researcher want to resubmit it to the same agency. The proposal-writing process is fraught with failure, but heeding review comments (responding to that discrete data point) works: the rate of funding for resubmitted proposals to the same agencies is typically higher (15–20 percent) than the overall funding rate because the author of the proposal has gone over the comments and has addressed problem areas accordingly.

Failure has also given me a thick skin, which makes it increasingly easier for me to keep trying. By sheer probability, the more times you try, the more times you succeed. While my ultimate goal is success, I know that navigating through and learning from my failures along the way is just as important.

Failure has taught me resolve, as well as the importance of being critical without being judgmental. Resolve is what led to getting funded on the tenth try for the Howell Park playground. Being critical of myself during that process ("Bolster your justification for a new playground and show more explicitly how the mission of the organization is directly served through this playground project.") instead of judgmental ("Lima, your ninth try was unsuccessful? Really? You must suck at writing proposals!") was what I needed to do to succeed.

The engineering profession is well versed in failure. Though the public tends to hear about major unintended failures, such as the Challenger space shuttle accident or the broken levees in New Orleans after Hurricane Katrina, engineering failures are generally expected. Engineers work with failure all the time, both in terms of probability (how long will something last before it fails) and in the design of devices and processes.

From a statistical standpoint, engineers view failure as inevitable: it is economically unrealistic to design something to last forever. Engineers could build cars or houses to last hundreds of years, but they would be so expensive that no one would be able to afford them. Failure is also inevitable because it is impossible to defy physical law and the second law of thermodynamics (that is, everything tends toward chaos). Think about a concrete slab that has been left alone for awhile. Weeds will fill in the cracks, and they will eventually overtake the concrete and break it down, until nothing is left but weeds and dirt. Even if the concrete slab is fastidiously maintained, eventually—due to wear and tear and changes in the concrete over time through exposure to weather, moisture, and so on—it will have to be repaired, and at some point, replaced.

Failure is also a major consideration in engineering design. The design process is iterative (repetitive) because engineers never get the design of an artifact or process right on the first try—we are always working to make it better. Professional writers will tell you that it is impossible to create a masterpiece with a first draft; they go through many drafts of a document before they get it right. Engineers are the same way with their designs. The first iteration of their design will not be a masterpiece, but maybe the eighth or tenth or hundredth iteration is the right design. To be a successful engineer, you have to be OK with trying and not succeeding. Somewhere along the way, my experiences with designing playgrounds and the instructive ways in which the engineering profession uses failure have led me to redefine my conception of failure. I believe that failure occurs when you stop trying. Failure occurs when you give up; it is not the opposite of success. Not being successful is not failing—it is normal operating procedure.

I try to reinforce these concepts to my students in as many ways as I can. My students are, by and large, terrified to fail; our culture is risk-averse and litigious, and students are aware of these facts. They also tend to carry high expectations of themselves, a feeling compounded by the expectations of their families, friends, and society.

I always tell my students that I am a success because I am an expert in failure as it is traditionally defined. Some of my failures have been high-stakes; I didn't get accepted to graduate school at Yale or the University of Michigan, even though I gave it my best shot. I did get in to Ohio State and Cornell; I went to Cornell and had a rough time there. I left Cornell twenty-one months after starting graduate school with no degree and an overwhelming feeling of failure. I spent a year recovering from this setback and getting up my nerve again before restarting my PhD at Ohio State. I remember feeling frustrated for taking so long to finish my degree; ultimately, I was almost four years behind my original, best-case plan. Being "behind" mattered a lot to me then. It doesn't anymore. I've learned that even with high-stakes failures, and even when you know that the goal that you're pursuing is not possible, you can change your goals in response to your setbacks and still get to the things that are important to you. The best things I took with me from my time at Cornell were the knowledge that I could land on my feet after a major setback and my peripheral involvement with the civil engineering club playground project, which planted the seed for the LSU Community Playground Project almost ten years later.

I also tell my students it's OK to fail if you define failure as not succeeding. I encourage them to fail within my classroom, and to fail with flair and gusto. Fail here and now so that you don't fail so much later: miss the calculation and crack the child's head open now, on your virtual playground, so that you don't later, on the actual playground. You are less likely to crack a child's head open in an actual situation if you made an error in the virtual world and learned from it. I am here to backstop any failure you might encounter on a playground design. If your first design doesn't work, use that data point to learn, collect, and analyze more information if you need to, and keep trying until your design works.

Working with community is similar to engineering design, because working with community involves working with incomplete information, constraints, and complexity. It is impossible to find workable solutions without setbacks. It is part of the territory. Embrace failure. Make friends with it.

Not being successful doesn't feel good, and there is no easy fix for that feeling. When I have to tell Principal Cheryl Lewis of White Hills Elementary that I once again did not secure funding for her school's playground, it feels awful. I am currently working on the sixth proposal for funding for White Hills, and this playground is starting to feel like Howell Park all over again. But my effort to bring in funding to get the White Hills playground built is not a failure. I just haven't succeeded yet. The steely resolve I've developed through multiple failures has taught me to use everything I've learned and continue to learn to improve my requests. The trick is to keep going and not to stop trying.

Follow Up When You Make a Mistake.

Upon first glance, this principle might seem like the previous one. In my mind, however, mistakes are not the same as failures. Mistakes are (usually) relatively small actions that you might "commit" when you're going fast and/or not thinking, or when you're not focused. I consider mistakes to be pseudo-failures. Mistakes can be tough, because while they may be little in terms of actions, they can have big consequences. I've also noticed that fear of making a mistake, especially saying or doing the wrong thing, is often enough of a barrier to stop people from engaging at all, especially around sensitive issues. I believe that it is critical to break through that barrier.

Just as everyone fails, everyone makes mistakes. You won't always say or do the correct thing. But I think that as long as your intention is good, you have a nose for knowing when you make a mistake, and you follow up with an honest effort to get things right, you've done as much as you can.

I've made many mistakes during my life. Here are three mistakes I've made on the playground project:

One: Years ago, I had a student named Ford Sutter in my playground design class. Ford was similar to my other students in terms of his great attitude and his interest in creating a first-rate playground design in conjunction with his community partner. One way in which Ford was different from my other students was that he was an amputee. His prosthetic was so well-fitted that I didn't know that he was an amputee until we took our first field trip to a local playground, when I ask my students to connect with the playground "as a child." I need my students to be able to ensure that their ultimate collaborative designs are fun, and I want them to re-experience this fun factor on a playground before they learn the safety standards that will forever change their conception of a playground (a process that begins later during the same field trip).

After running around the playground and trying every available play activity, Ford took off his prosthetic leg and proceeded to repeat his journey around the playground while hopping instead of running. Ford whooped the entire time, whether playing on one foot or two.

My favorite part of that day was watching the rest of my students watch Ford play at 100 percent capacity after he removed his prosthetic leg. It can be hard to convey to students that you don't simplify a playground to provide access for people with disabilities. Just as my students tend to think that the sole thing you need to provide an adult caregiver on a playground is a place to sit (wrong!), they tend to think that passive activities are the only things on a playground you need to provide for a child with disabilities (wrong again!). I truly believe I watched that notion be entirely dispensed with as I tracked my students' facial reactions while watching Ford vigorously engage in every play activity on the play space. He may have needed properly placed railings to access every play activity, but the railings were there because the playground we visited that day was ADA accessible. Ford made great use of the railings and taught my students an indelible lesson about the importance of accessibility that day. Within a two-minute period, designing for accessibility was not about "them" (a child with disabilities) but about "us" (a person in our class).

Ford successfully completed my class and, like many of my former students, continued to drop by my office occasionally to say hello and to ask about the status of the latest playground. He happened to drop by on a day when I was mired in a thunderstorm of work. We commiserated for a minute with his school schedule and my work one, and then he asked, "Are you OK?"

"Well," I replied, "at least I'm standing on two feet." I used this figure of speech often, and I meant that while I had a lot on my plate, I was still standing (versus swimming or drowning in work).

"At least you have two feet," Ford said. I looked him straight in the eyes, and I knew that he clearly saw the "Oh, that was insensitive of me" look plastered across my face.

"Gotcha, Doc," he said, and we both burst out laughing. I appreciated Ford's humorous, tactful way of reminding me of the importance of language, and of keeping a work load in proper perspective. I've since ceased using my "two feet" statement—there are better ways to express the sentiment of feeling overloaded with work tasks.

Two: I was essentially fired once by a community partner based on a miscommunication involving the media. My team and I had met twice with the school. We had collected design ideas from the school community and were ready to start the playground design process when we were approached by a local TV news channel for a story about the collaboration. The school principal wanted to publicize all parts of the playground design process through the media and had made this fact clear to me during our face-to-face meetings, so when we got a call from the TV station, and the reporter mentioned that the school principal had given her my contact information, my team and I assented to being interviewed. The TV crew came and took footage during one of our team meetings, in which we reviewed sketches that my students had created of the existing playground and began brainstorming for the new playground design.

The ninety-second story aired a couple of days after our interview. I had not yet seen it when I received a call from the principal, who had viewed it and was furious.

"How dare you show a preliminary playground design for our school to the media that we haven't seen first?" she screamed. "I'm thinking of cutting you out of our project right now. We can find someone else to work with us!"

It was difficult to respond when I hadn't seen the story, and I was so taken aback at the principal's vitriol that I apologized profusely and multiple times, stated our interest in continuing the collaboration and asked what I could do to ensure our continuing relationship.

"I will not fire you based on one condition and one condition only," she barked, "that you never, *ever,* talk to the media about our project again."

"OK," I said, and she hung up.

I practiced a little deep breathing and went in search of the TV segment. I watched it multiple times and was pleased with the way in which the story had portrayed the mutual partnership between the school and the playground design team. Yet, sure enough, the story presented my team's drawings of the school's current playground as new playground design concepts. It was a mistake from which our partnership never recovered.

One of the best pieces of advice I ever got was this: "If the media gets 70 percent of your story correct, that's about the best you can hope for." I've found this statement to be pretty true. I am not blaming the media; with the speed at which news moves, it is easy to miss nuance. Generally, reporters have time for only the high points of a story; with such a focus, it is easy to overlook details or context. Even if details and context are contained in a story, they may be removed during editing due to time or space constraints. One important thing to remember with the media is this: if there are major errors in media stories, address them by contacting the media source and providing corrections. Media sources will make changes accordingly, either through errata in newsprint or by editing past and future broadcasts.

I shared my issue with Jan Shoemaker, the director of LSU's Center for Community Engagement, Learning, and Leadership, and she told me that the media is the most common cause of conflict between university and community partners. Typical pitfalls include a focus on one-way helping (with the university helping the community) instead of two-way collaboration (community and university working together), or with community partners and their contributions being overlooked in the media. She gave me the great suggestion of having a media plan in place with every partnership, with all parties having the same talking points. She also suggested frequent communication among constituencies regarding the media, and whenever possible, ensuring that partnership constituencies be interviewed together.

My students and I completed an initial design and corresponding bid specifications of the school playground shortly after the TV story aired, and I contacted the principal to schedule a time for us to come to present it and to get feedback to fine-tune the design. She told me to email the design and specifications so that she and the school improvement team could see them first. I sent the requested information and never received a response. I followed up several times to ensure that the school had received the design before realizing that the non-response was in and of itself a clear form of communication.

I was contacted by purchasing staff at the parish school board office a couple of times to provide additional details on the bid specifications, so I knew that the design had been submitted to purchasing by the school. However, I never heard from the school again. The company that ultimately installed our collaborative design (the school elected not to use a community build) sent us pictures of the completed playground. We were not invited to the ribbon cutting.

This miscommunication represents a big mistake with the playground project. I did make an effort to try to resolve my community partner's concern, and although the conflict was not resolved in a way in which I am comfortable, as a result I have been much more careful with the media. Whenever possible, we try to have all constituencies interviewed together, and our ensuing partnerships have been strengthened by addressing the mistakes we encountered during this derailed project.

Three: I made a mistake on the Twin Oaks playground, which actually involved two new playgrounds, one for older children (grades 1–5) and one for kindergartners. Playground design is split into different age groups to ensure that children are matched with activities appropriate for their developmental levels. In terms of play, there are three age groups: toddlers (6–23 months old), preschool-age children (2–5 years old), and school-age children (5–12 years old). There is an overlap at age 5 to indicate that some students are more developmentally advanced than others. A major consideration in four- to five-year-olds is upper body strength, so in designing playgrounds for that age range, you need to make sure that there aren't climbers or other upper body activities that the children won't be able to handle.

When my students and I worked with the Twin Oaks community to design the kindergarten playground, we were thinking about providing a range of challenge to the children. The idea is that you provide different ways for kids to swing, slide, spin, balance, climb, and brachiate (swing with your arms from handhold to handhold). Some of these ways might be easy, while others might be more difficult. For example, children could reach a platform on a playground by climbing steps, which is easier, or by climbing a ladder, which is harder. We considered the kindergartners to be school-age children and while generally we didn't choose the hardest methods for children to engage physically, we did provide a couple of challenges.

The biggest challenge we included was a fire pole. A fire pole is one of my favorite activities to put on a playground for numerous reasons. It provides a great way for children to engage in imaginative play. I've seen children use a fire pole as a fire pole (they're fireman going to put out a fire), but also as a racer (they time themselves to see who can get to the top the fastest), as a quick way to get from the "ship" to the "water," and as a fun stop on an obstacle course, in which a child stands on top of the platform and another child shimmies up the pole and tags the child on the platform (or grabs a beanbag strategically placed on the platform) in order to proceed to the next obstacle course activity. Sliding down or climbing up a fire pole is challenging in a way that gym teachers absolutely love; the almost universal complaint we hear from physical education teachers is a lack of upper body strength in their students and a corresponding lack of equipment to enable children to develop this strength. Another great thing about fire poles is their proverbial bang for the buck. A fire pole is one of the cheapest playground components available. Because of this combination of factors, fire poles find their way onto most of our playgrounds.

Placing a fire pole on a kindergartner's playground was a stretch, admittedly. We knew that not all students in a kindergarten class would be able to use it; in fact, probably only a fraction of them would be able to use it initially. But given the numerous other activities available on the playground, we felt the fire pole was OK to include. It would give kids something to shoot for that everyone could aspire to use.

The Twin Oaks collaboration was a fantastic one, with engaged elementary school students and teachers, a committed principal, my students, me, and Joe all working together with executives from Lowe's who generously funded both playgrounds and all the surfacing that went with them. We had our typical checks and balances in place, and although there was a hitch during the two-day build with a couple of improperly shipped equipment components that hindered the completion of one of the playgrounds, the job was completed smoothly. The installer finished the second playground the following week, after the proper equipment components were received.

I felt great about this playground. I felt especially great about the fact that the kindergarten playground was the one with the portal to anywhere, and that the kids on that playground now had awesome equipment to go with it. My satisfaction turned to horror when the principal contacted me and said that the playground couldn't pass ECERS-R because of the fire pole, and possibly some other climbing equipment as well. It was not until this phone call that I realized that what I had thought of as a kindergarten playground was actually a playground for kindergartners and pre-kindergartners, kids who are four years old. A fire pole should absolutely not be used by a four-year-old. Other pieces of equipment were in question, but after checking safety guidelines, all of it was approved for use by children four years old and older.

I was shocked I had made a mistake about the age range of this playground and that even with our checks and balances in place, none of us caught the error. I contacted Joe to apologize. Joe's first instinct was to be upset with the company that received our bid, but I told him not to be upset with them because the error was mine. The company had delivered exactly what we had specified, and we had specified a fire pole. I told Joe I'd pay to have the pole removed and replaced with something else. He told me not to worry about it and that Aramark would take care of it. Meanwhile, the Twin Oaks community addressed the issue by not allowing pre-kindergarten students to play on the fire pole.

I felt confident that I'd been told the wrong information about what age group this playground was supposed to serve. My confidence dissolved when I went back and reread my notes from our initial meetings with the Twin Oaks staff. My notes clearly said in several places that the playground was intended for pre-kindergarten and kindergarten students.

This mistake bothered me because it was a pretty basic error that I had made without ever realizing it, and one that our design checks didn't catch. I forgave myself for making this mistake; every school splits their playground in a different way, and not every school has a pre-kindergarten program. I was working with at least six different schools at the time, so it was easy to mix up playgrounds and age groups. But in the spirit of Atul Gawande and his immensely useful book *The Checklist Manifesto,* I also created a new check in our system: after the finalized design is agreed upon, I recheck with the school principal and with Aramark to ensure that the age range of the children is commensurate with the playground equipment.

Mistakes tend to bother me more than failures do, probably because they feel more within my power to stop before they occur in the first place. I try to remember what Jan Shoemaker always says: the only people who aren't making mistakes are the ones who aren't doing anything. We are human beings, and making mistakes is inevitable and a normal part of living. The key is addressing mistakes when you make them and being willing to keep those mistakes in perspective.

Yes, I once said that I have two feet to a person who has one. Yes, I once was essentially fired for not checking with a community partner before giving an interview to the media. And yes, I specified a piece of playground equipment specifically not intended for some of the children regularly using that playground. These are a few of the many mistakes I have made.

What is the end result of those mistakes? Ford Sutter is out there spreading joy in the world. The playground misrepresented in media was built and is now used by almost six hundred children every school day. The Twin Oaks playground now serves some sixty pre-kindergarten and kindergarten students every day sans fire pole. I am more careful about the language I use to ensure that I don't offend people. I make every effort to involve my community partners directly every time we have a request from the media. Finally, I triple-check the grade levels and corresponding ages of the children who will play on our collaborative playgrounds to ensure the proper age group has access to the proper equipment.

As much as I dislike making mistakes, fixing them has made me a more aware person, and at the end of the day, I believe that being more aware is a good thing. I know that I haven't made my last mistake, but I also know that making mistakes is an inevitable part of life. When I make a mistake, I own it, apologize, and make an effort to address it.

Don't Take No for an Answer.

If you endeavor to do anything within a community and you are working on something complex, you will probably hear no a lot. Similar expressions of skepticism go something like this:

- Oh, I don't think so.
- That's impossible.
- You can't do that.
- But that's not how we do things.

- No one's ever done this before.
- You want to do what?
- Are you nuts?
- Ha, ha, ha, ha, ha!!!

Working on playgrounds "in the spaces in between," with one foot in the university and one in the community, has taught me that systems are set up to do routine business. If your project does not fit into an institutional culture in a routine way, you are likely to hear no or similar sentiments quite a bit.

I've heard varieties of no so many times that I've entitled this phenomenon my "no one's ever done this before" virtual playground: if I had a dollar for every time someone has told me some version of no, I'd be able to build a playground with the money. I'm guessing it's in the range of $30,000. The trick is to not stop in the face of no.

People who say no almost always do so without malice and usually want to work with you as much as they can. Part of this phenomenon is due to the culture of south Louisiana, where most people will give you the shirt off their back if you ask them for it, but part of it is people in general. And so I've learned that while I might hear no a lot, I won't stop with no for an answer.

I've found that if I ask why the answer is no, and I ask why respectfully, there will be a specific reason underlying the no. And if I can figure out a way to address that specific reason, the no almost always goes away.

Here are some examples. If you've ever watched the movie *A Christmas Story*, you are familiar with the mother–BB gun theme. In the movie, nine-year-old protagonist Ralphie wants a BB gun for Christmas, but his mother is convinced that he will shoot his eye out with a BB gun and is determined that Santa will not bring him his heart's desire. I've experienced parallel phenomena to the mother's resistance to a BB gun from both principals and teachers.

Teachers and administrators are vigilant about the safety of their children, and rightly so. I've had principals and teachers say things like, "Three of my children broke their wrists last year on a monkey bar before I had it removed, and I won't have another set of monkey bars on my playground!" I respectfully ask if the monkey bar was surfaced, and the answer is usually no (if yes, the surfacing was not maintained at the proper depth). I explain that if the equipment is properly surfaced and the amount of surfacing is properly maintained, then the chances decrease dramatically of a child breaking a wrist on a monkey bar or getting hurt by falling from a swing. The teachers and principals always listen to me, as I always listen to them. Sometimes they allow the equipment back onto the playground (or allow it to stay if the surfacing is upgraded and maintained properly), and sometimes they won't.

I will typically not push a no like this because it is a matter of respecting my community partners and their wishes. I make sure that principals and teachers have all the information they need to make the decision that works best for their school. Sometimes these decisions are thorny because a school might have one or two outspoken teachers against having a particular piece of equipment on their playground while the principal and/or the gym teacher are in favor of acquiring that equipment. In my experience, schools embody the best of democracy in these situations, because they have well-established methods for hearing everyone's opinion and then having a group of people—such as a school improvement team or a playground planning team—analyze everyone's input and make a transparent, fair, informed decision.

While I will not actively try to discourage a community partner from saying no, I will try to negotiate a no from a funding agency or from a system within a bureaucracy. In *A Christmas Story*, Ralphie finds another route to Santa for his BB gun through his dad. Throughout my experiences with community engagement, I've made copious use of alternative routes. Those routes—whether proposal resubmissions, proposals to different parts of the same organization, or alternative ways to get things done while still adhering to the rules—are what have enabled playgrounds to be built, and recess to exist when it hadn't before. My philosophy in this regard is "water on rock." Glacial progress is still progress; if I never stop going (like water), eventually I will wear away any resistance (the rock).

Sometimes there is a limit on what can be done in the face of no. Sometimes the answer truly is no, and nothing can be done to change it. One has to know when to stop trying to make the no turn into a maybe or a yes. I will stop in any situation when I hear what Professor Lesia Crumpton-Young has termed the "Texas version of a final answer," which is, "HELL NO, AND DON'T ASK ME AGAIN."

Until you hear that, and as long as you are being properly respectful of and honest with your community partners in the process, I'd keep working on negotiating through a no. In my more than ten years of working with community, I've heard the Texas version of a no only twice.

It's OK to Be Overwhelmed.

The longer I've worked with my community on playgrounds, the more I've fallen behind on getting them finished. Some playgrounds, like Brusly, River Oaks, and Jefferson Terrace, have been fast from start to finish. Others, like Howell Park and Sharon Hills, have been slow to come to fruition. I realize that even with my best efforts, I have gotten to (and have most likely surpassed) my full capacity. I truly can't do any more than I'm doing now, and still there is need that I simply cannot address. At this point, my team is working on about eight playground designs simultaneously, and each of my team members is the lead project manager on at least one playground. The playgrounds are literally coming faster than we can keep up with them. In this situation, it's easy to get overwhelmed. The dean of LSU's College of Agriculture, Ken Koonce, likes to say, "If you're not behind, it means you're not doing enough." I appreciate his sentiment, but being behind and feeling overwhelmed never is 100 percent comfortable.

Chances are that if you have been working to address a community issue for an extended period of time, you have felt overwhelmed either intermittently or as a general state of being. While it's easy to say, "Don't be overwhelmed," it's often hard to stop feeling that way. When I'm feeling overwhelmed, I remind myself to do four things.

First, I remember to delegate. I've found over the course of my life that there are lessons I've had to learn only once, and lessons I've had to learn again and again. Delegation is one of those "over and over" lessons. I know that delegation works; the playground project is successful in large part because we share the workload among the elementary school, the college students, Aramark, and community volunteers. We have accomplished extraordinary things by working together to do ordinary things. I know that I'm not doing everything, but if someone asks me to do something, I tend to say yes and I tend to think about doing it myself instead of asking someone else. When that number of things swells my to-do list to longer than a single-spaced page, I tend to get overwhelmed, so I need to step back, remind myself of the power of delegation, and match people and tasks accordingly.

Second, I try to remember good time-management techniques. There's a lot of good, public information about time management, so I will share the one technique from which I've gotten the most mileage. Out of all the things you're doing right now, one is the most important. Whatever that most important thing is, spend at least 25 percent of your free, unscheduled time doing it. For example, if I have a 40-hour work week and 16 hours of that week are spent in class and in meetings, I have 24 hours of unscheduled work time. My most important work project, whatever it is, should get my attention at least 6 hours that week, and every subsequent week, until it is finished. When it's done, I then assign another project as my most important project and continue.

The trick to getting this technique to work is to ensure that the time you commit to your most important project is good, efficient time without distraction. Sometimes my most important project doesn't take 100 percent of my concentration, but most of the time, it does. My best concentration time occurs in my home office, where there are no people, no cell phones (I turn mine off or at least put it on vibrate), and no emails. Make sure that you reserve your most important project time, and treat that time with as much reverence as you would a meeting with the President.

Third, I remember to eat the frog. I love what I do, but in any job, volunteer or otherwise, there are sometimes unpleasant or burdensome tasks. On these tasks, I tend to procrastinate. The stress from not doing things I should do (or should have already completed) contributes immensely to my feeling overwhelmed. Eating the frog is a catchphrase for doing the dreaded task and doing it now. Eat that frog! While it may not taste good, everything coming afterwards tastes better. In other words, it's easier to do all the other things you need to do once you've finished the dreaded thing you had to do.

I told my friend Roxanne about this concept and she said, "What if everything you do is a frog?" Roxanne lived in a village in rural Africa for a time, and she told me that in the evenings, frogs would gather symphony-style in semicircular rows in front of cottage doors and would literally serenade the cottage occupants. When villagers flung open their doors, they would be greeted by hundreds of pairs of eyes and a cacophony of croaks and ribbits. The frogs were attracted to the lights in the cottages. Roxanne said that those frog symphonies reminded her of her own personal version of eat the frog. When you're in a perpetual state of being behind, it does start to seem like everything is a frog. She and I laughed about those frogs; we laugh a little about everything. We constantly battle frogs, but we take the time to talk about our frogs over lunch at least once a semester.

My fourth and final reminder is this: Remember that you are not the only one out there who is overwhelmed. Every community has a trench, a place in which people hunker down to work for the common good. When you feel overwhelmed, reach out to the people who are in that trench with you so you can feel overwhelmed together. The commiseration is useful, but the support you give each other is precious. I leave every lunch I have with Roxanne renewed. It's not that I'm any less behind than I was before lunch; it's just that after speaking with her, I'm OK with stuff getting done when it gets done.

Let Go, Because Control Is an Illusion—But Also Hang On, Because You Have Some Influence.

One of the playground rules in Chapter 3 was to watch for unintended consequences. For example, pea gravel used as a playground safety surfacing material resulted in broken vacuum cleaners, because after children inadvertently tracked the gravel inside, the custodial staff vacuumed it up and it broke the machines. Even though I try to be prepared for anything, it is impossible to control all the outcomes of any given situation; moreover, there are some things impossible to see coming. Janet Eyler's statement about community-engaged work bears repeating: "Complexity is not a problem, it's a feature."

If you work with community for a long time, situations will present themselves in which you will not have an easy or straightforward course of action. You will also not have control over the ultimate outcomes. Having been faced with this state of affairs multiple times, I have come to the conclusion that control is an illusion, and that the best thing to do is to roll with it, to do my best to provide a positive attitude, and, when possible, to exert a positive influence.

The playground we built at the McMains Children's Developmental Center was our fourth playground and our largest playground at the time. It took several weeks to complete all the preparatory construction work for this playground, which included raising the elevation of the play area almost a foot to make the playground less susceptible to flooding. Because the playground was specifically designed for children with disabilities, we specified unitary surfacing material (USM) on as much of the playground as we could afford. USM is wheelchair accessible and is spread road-style (like laying down the layers of a road) by professionals after the play equipment has been installed. Weeks in advance, playground company Agrestics and McMains executive director Janet Ketcham had ordered the play equipment and had secured the surfacing company to spread the surfacing after the play equipment was installed. The play equipment order was delayed more than once and finally arrived on site on Friday, September 6, 2002. The surfacing company was set to begin installing the USM on Monday morning, September 9, 2002. We had to install the equipment over the weekend in order to be ready for the surfacing company; if we were not ready, the surfacing company would charge a $2,000 penalty for rescheduling, and none of us had that extra cash. Luckily, we had plenty of time and lots of volunteers, so installation over the weekend was not a major issue.

Enter Tropical Storm Fay. Almost no one has ever heard of Tropical Storm Fay, which caused some property damage, mostly in Texas, but which was generally benign enough that the National Hurricane Center recycled the name, as it does on a six-year rotation, when a storm causes no significant damage or death. (There was another Tropical Storm Fay in 2008, which caused much more property damage than in 2002). Tropical Storm Fay's 2002 incarnation may have been a blip on most people's radar, but for those of us who volunteered that weekend on the McMains playground, it is a storm we will never forget. We worked two, long, full days and it never once stopped raining. The good news was that the temperature was pleasant; the bad news was that the work was slowed by the steady, incessant rain. One of my student volunteers brought a red, inflatable frog to the site, who we nicknamed Fay and who served as our mascot for the weekend. We erected a small tent next to the Agrestics supply truck to stand under to eat and to take short breaks from the rain. Mostly, we slogged through the installation of swings and a composite structure while soaked to the bone. We finished the job at about 6 p.m. on Sunday. The surfacing crew showed up first thing Monday morning to an absolutely gorgeous, sunny day and began their two-day job.

In this situation, there was not a single thing I could do to change or control Tropical Storm Fay. I did my best to keep everyone's spirits up—in other words, to positively influence what I could—but in this case, as in many cases, I decided to let go (and get wet) because control is an illusion. We did the best we could with the situation at hand, and ultimately we were successful. The job was finished on time without a $2,000 penalty. There were lots of soaked volunteers and soggy cars, but that was OK too.

The community playgrounds we've collectively created tend to be gathering places in which community members take pride. Early on, I'd get infrequent phone calls from frustrated principals or teachers who would tell me that someone had taken basketball nets from their basketball hoops, or trees and plants from their school garden, or playground safety surfacing from under their play equipment. I understood their frustration and quickly adopted a "stubborn in the face of adversity" stance when faced with this rare, unfortunate situation. Now, we prepare to get a little extra. A new mesh net for a basketball hoop costs about $2.50; it's almost as easy to buy ten as it is to buy one. So we buy ten. If someone takes down a net, we put up another one. If someone takes a tree, we plant another one in its place. If a person takes some mulch, we spread some more. We may not be able to control this situation, but collectively we exert a positive influence on it and send this message to everyone: The positive, dynamic community space created by many people is too important to be destroyed by the actions of a few.

Yes, control is an illusion. Letting go of the idea of control is also good; you can't stop a person who will take something from a community site. However, you do have a sphere of influence. Remember to hang on to that and to use it. Too many times, I have seen the actions of one anonymous person ruin the collective efforts of hundreds of people to improve a community. I've decided that I am not going to spend any time lamenting the actions of that one anonymous person; instead, I'm going to respond proactively. I'm going to work with others to locate the resources to address this rare issue. I believe in the goodness of people; I know that the vast majority of people do not take from the collective creation of others. I will use my sphere of influence to reinforce the maxim that the good will of the community and its work together is bigger than the actions of one person.

Take Care of Yourself!

As with making friends with failure, the importance of this concept cannot be overemphasized. If you endeavor to do anything significant over the long haul within your community, you have to take care of yourself along the way or you will not be successful. I take care of myself; it's the reason that I can stay positive in the face of my "no one's ever done this before" virtual playground. It's why my philosophy of glacial progress with water on rock works. If I didn't take care of myself, my water would evaporate from the rock due to pure exhaustion. I am confident that you know how to take care of yourself simply by virtue of reading this book. Here are some reminders that may help.

- Make sure you get enough sleep. Contrary to popular belief, you do not need less sleep as you get older!
- Set aside times during each week that are always, absolutely your own. During these times, do the things that rejuvenate you.
- Make a list of all the things you do to relax. Place this list in prominent places so you will encounter it and be reminded of it. Regularly do things on the list. Periodically add five items to your list that you're interested in or always thought you might like to do, and do them too.
- Take up a hobby if you don't have one already. Here are some examples of hobbies practiced by community fire plugs I know: acting, archery, bird watching, belly dancing, Cajun dancing, fishing, gardening, hiking (while leaving no trace on the ecosystem), joining a game club, reading trash novels, making regular trips to nature, joining recre-

ational sports leagues, photography, sign language, travel, triathlons, walking, yoga.

- Take a break. My yoga teacher, Carmen Board, will often say to her roomful of pupils as we get started with a series of highly energetic yoga moves, "If you get tired, wait for us in child's pose (a relaxation pose). We'll keep going, but we're always here with you. Just find us again when you're ready to join us." Community-engaged work is also like that. If you need to rest, do it. We're still here with you; just jump back in and find us when you're ready.
- Remember to have fun! If you haven't played lately for the sheer fun of it, try it! My favorite fun activity on a playground is a zip line. What's yours?

I am of the opinion that my life belongs to the whole community and as long as I live, it is my privilege to do for it whatever I can. I want to be thoroughly used up when I die, for the harder I work the more I live.

—George Bernard Shaw

Getting Involved
Advice from Community Fire Plugs

Welcome! Whether you plan to spend a total of two hours engaged with your community, or two hours a week for the rest of your life, your contribution is necessary, important, and appreciated. Becoming an engaged citizen can be a critically important way to address community issues and to serve people in need.

As I began sketching out this chapter, I realized that its message would be much stronger with many voices instead of just my own. With that idea in mind, I invited together a number of community leaders with whom I share the trench and asked them to engage in a ninety-minute discussion on community—specifically, on what advice they would give to someone looking to become involved in their community. The conversations we had together in large and small groups form the basis of this chapter.

These leaders are involved in their communities in multiple capacities. Some have devoted their careers to community engagement as service-learning teachers, ministers, or employees of nonprofit organizations. All have significant experience as volunteers. Their perspectives are informed by their varied experiences and lends to the collective wisdom shared in this chapter. These leaders, whom I deeply thank for their contributions, are: Sharon Williams Andrews, Christy Kayser Arrazattee, Judy Bethly, Carolyn

Carnahan, Blythe Daigle, Jenola Duke, Blaine Grimes, Betsy Irvine, Kristin Mensen, Deborah Normand, Janet Pace, Cindy Seghers, Jan Shoemaker, Phyllis Simpson, Karen Stagg, Mallory Trochesset, and Liz Wyatt.

We have a number of suggestions for going about getting involved in your community. Some of this information is about you and some is about your community. We wish you the best of luck on your journey of service.

It is possible to contribute spontaneously to your community by simply showing up and offering your services. Some of us got our initial start in this manner, or because community service was required by our school or church, or because a friend or family member asked us to join their cause. Although all these approaches can work, your experience will probably be more meaningful to you and to your community if you do a little planning before getting involved. We suggest the following approach:

- Find your passion.
- Identify your talent.
- Search community organizations to find a match for your passion and talent.
- Contact your match(es) and choose your partner volunteer organization(s).
- Engage! Get out there and do it!

Find your passion. Ultimately, we believe that it's important to get involved in something about which you care deeply. If you care about an issue, a cause, or a group of people, you are more likely to share your heart and soul in service to that issue, and that's important, because we need all of you to contribute. When you bring concentrated energy to the table, and others do as well, the positive outcomes of your work together are greatly enhanced. That's what Margaret Mead meant when she wrote, "Never doubt that a thoughtful group of committed citizens can change the world. Indeed, it's the only thing that ever has."

A partial list of the passions held by us include: enhancing adult and child literacy; improving the quality of public education; promoting financial literacy; eliminating predatory lending; advocating for children through groups such as Court Appointed Special Advocates (CASA) and Grandparents Raising Grandchildren; ensuring a safe, productive transition of women from prison to society; addressing racial inequality; providing clean water to people throughout the world; advocating for animals; providing affordable access to high-quality health care; addressing obesity issues; ensuring a sustainable ecosystem for all living species; and organizing volunteers around systemic issues such as poverty (through the service commission of the state, for example).

Mallory Trochesset says of herself, "Honestly, I am still figuring out my passion for service and the community. I see so many colleagues, peers, and mentors who have that one social issue or cause that they fight for; however, I don't feel as though I fit into that paradigm. I truly believe that my passion is working with college students and instilling within them the desire to be responsible citizens. For me, I believe that every person makes a difference, and that it is through our shared action that we make change happen. If I can help each college student identify their own passion and take action on it, think of what a better world this might be! It inspires me daily."

You may have many passions or you may have no passions. Don't worry; either way, there is a place for you in the community. Most of us have many passions and we've had to go through the difficult but necessary process of focusing our efforts. There is only so much a single person can do, and while it is easy to multiply your efforts by working with others, there are also only so many hours in the day. So many causes, so little time! We tend to handle this overload by prioritizing our time and energy and focusing on what we care about most. There are many ways to contribute to important causes and organizations; we might give money to certain organizations while contributing our time and energy (and maybe some funds as well) to others.

If you have no passions, that's OK too. We encourage you to think about experiences in your life that you really enjoyed and the people, places, and purposes that pertain to those experiences. You might get clues regarding what you care about from your past experiences; use them to start to brainstorm ideas about how you'd like to contribute to community. You can also ask influential people in your life how and why they got involved in community; you will probably hear some really interesting stories you've never heard before, and you may well find kernels of ideas that will connect with your own interests. What's remarkable about this process is that as you begin your search for a passion, sometimes that passion finds you instead, without you even realizing it. Many of us have gone in directions we never imagined because a passion picked us instead of the other way around.

Identify your talents. You will make the strongest contribution to your community if you are able to use your talents in a service capacity. We are confident that by virtue of reading this information, you do in fact possess talents. Your talents may involve skill sets (like communication) or personality traits (like tenacity).

There are many ways that a volunteer's skill sets and traits can be used in a service capacity. For example, in a community-based playground build, children provide their expertise in play, hospitality volunteers use their people skills to orient other volunteers to the site and assign them to teams, construction volunteers contribute their knowledge of tools and building, strong volunteers bring their brawn to move and spread heavy, shock-absorbing material under and around play equipment, culinary volunteers use their cooking expertise to provide meals for everyone, and project management volunteers use their organizational skills systematically to monitor the site to ensure that all volunteers are safe, comfortable, and on-task. A number of skill sets and traits are at work in this example of episodic service. Whether you are involved in short- or long-term service, your unique set of skills and personality traits can be useful to a community organization, especially if you can articulate them to the organization early on and then share them in a service capacity.

Many community organizations function with a shortage of resources and people and an excess of needs to address. Almost every community organization needs volunteers to help write proposals for funding, to assist in fundraising efforts, and to maintain and update computer hardware, software, and online material (for example, a website). Generally, computer and writing skills are highly prized by community organizations. If you possess these skills, we suggest that you mention your talents in these areas with community groups during your initial meetings.

Some volunteer agencies will train you to provide you with the skill sets necessary to execute a service activity safely and efficiently, but other organizations may not. Typically, a community organization will start by assigning you small, manageable tasks; you tend to move up to more important tasks as you prove yourself and demonstrate your commitment to the organization or cause.

Sometimes you might think that your skill sets are not being effectively used. Please realize that generally you can't begin your service to an organization by starting as its leader. Remember to enjoy yourself: take your time, learn the organization, develop relationships with people in your community, give 100 percent of your effort to every task you are assigned, and look for ways to contribute your skill sets and traits to the mission of the organization with whom you are serving.

Search community organizations to find a match for your passion and talent. Once you've found your passion (or are in the process of doing so) and identified your talents, it's time to gather information about the communities in which you plan to serve and the organizations with whom you'd like to collaborate. Most communities—be they neighborhoods, schools, campuses, towns, cities, counties, parishes, or states—have a network of volunteer organizations; some organizations have national or international umbrellas. It would be useful for you to learn the lay of the land with respect to major volunteer organizations, their missions, and the ways in which they connect to communities around the world. See the Appendix entitled "Volunteer Organizations" for more information.

We suggest connecting with your local organizing volunteer networks to get started on identifying good prospects for community service. We've noticed that some Americans who think about service work initially consider other countries because they assume that there is need in other countries that does not exist within their community or within the United States. We strongly believe in international service because we believe that all nations are connected in humanity. There is tremendous need internationally. Approximately half of the seven billion people on this planet live on less than $2 a day, and many of these people have no access to clean water, food, shelter, or health care. But we also strongly believe in local volunteering. Tremendous need can often be found within a mile of where you reside.

Once you've identified the service organizations in which you're interested, see if you can locate additional information about the organization before approaching them directly. Most organizations have information online or in print format that details their mission, vision, and volunteer programs. Collecting more information is useful because in learning more about the organization, you will develop a clearer understanding of whether or not you want to work with them.

You may discover that your interest in serving may not be met through a typical community organization. You might consider volunteering online: both virtual volunteering and microvolunteering are becoming more popular. Virtual volunteering involves completing volunteer tasks online to benefit a nonprofit organization. Microvolunteering is a type of virtual volunteering that involves performing easy tasks on a short-term basis to benefit the common good.

You might also consider volunteering directly in the community but outside the confines of a community organization. Being a citizen in your own community—in other words, being neighborly—is important to the vitality of every community. We are reminded of the concept of neighborliness because of hurricane season, which has the Baton Rouge community on alert six months of every year. Perhaps, like ours, your local community is affected by hurricanes, or by other natural disasters such as floods, tornadoes, or wildfires. Natural disasters tend to keep you on your toes in terms of making sure that the people in your immediate community are OK. However, you don't need a natural disaster or the threat of one to reach out to a person down the block who may need a lawn to be mowed, a garden to be weeded, a ride to the grocery store, or even just a smile, a wave, and a hello.

Contact your matches and choose your partner volunteer organizations. Once you've gathered information about prospective volunteer organization(s) and put it together with your talents and your passion, you should contact the organization(s) to discuss potential partnerships. Together, you can come up with a better idea of how you could contribute your time, talents, and energy to the organization. It's important both for you and the organization that the match between you is a positive, workable one. Remember that the matching process is a two-way street; both you and the organization will decide whether or not you will work together.

Through their literature or websites, many organizations make clear that they have a preferred mode of communication; we strongly suggest that you contact the service organization in the way that they prefer. We suggest that you provide your name, your interest in the organization and in learning more about how to serve it effectively, and your contact information, including the best times and ways to reach you. Wait for a response from the organization if you don't get an answer immediately. Remember that many organizations are understaffed and may not be able to get to your communication for at least seventy-two hours. We do suggest that you follow up after about a week if you haven't heard anything.

Once you make contact with the organization, whether by phone or face to face, ask questions to ensure that there is a good match between the service needs of the organization and your talents and interests. For example,

- I have experience with [list your talents and skill sets]; can I make use of these experiences in a service capacity with your organization? If so, how?
- How can I best serve your organization?
- I would like to commit [X hours] per week to this organization by coming to your location every [suggest a day and time]. Is this a workable schedule?

We cannot overemphasize the importance of asking questions, not just about the organization, but also about the community and the people it serves. Professor Talmage Stanley says, "We often walk in with answers when we don't even know the questions yet." You serve most effectively when you know and understand your community. Ask questions before suggesting ideas or solutions.

Respect for the community is essential for long-term, transformative community service, and it is respectful to contribute our time, talents, energy, and experiences while learning about and being respectful of the time, talents, energy, and experiences of others. Asking questions is a great way to learn about the community and to begin to develop the relationships, flexibility, and trust that will enable you to effectively serve within your community.

Remember that the main focus of making contact is to ensure that there's a strong match between you and the community organization regarding your prospective service. There may not be a strong match between your interests and talents and those of a prospective community organization. If this is the case, it's perfectly fine for you or the organization to conclude that you should contribute elsewhere. On this point, Jan Shoemaker, community leader and proper southern lady, says, "You don't have to go home with everyone you dance with. If there's not a good fit between you and the organization, try something else!"

Engage! Get out there and do it! Once you've completed all your research and have chosen the ways in which you will engage with community, you're ready to jump into it! We hope that you will join us, and that you have fun and receive great satisfaction throughout your journeys in service.

We have several recommendations on getting started. The first is to recruit a buddy. This could be someone you already know who you think will enjoy the service experience, in which case you could ask him or her to join you, or it could be someone you meet within the context of your service experience. It's always useful to have a buddy with whom to share your thoughts, ideas, feelings, and experiences concerning your work with community. You will probably have experiences that make you feel truly happy and content, and others which might dismay and/or shock you. In the latter cases particularly, it's great to have a buddy with service experience to speak to.

The second recommendation is to make service a habit, what Alexis de Toqueville deemed "a habit of the heart." It is our experience that engagement in service over time is the type of effort that truly makes lasting, positive change. Community leader Mallory Trochesset says, "The human connection is powerful, and it is when we create meaningful relationships with those around us that we find ourselves truly 'hooked' to service. It is through these strong relationships—getting to know the agency staff and their challenges or understanding the experiences and stories of the people we are serving—that we truly grasp the depth of the service and our role in having a positive impact that will transform the lives of others."

The last recommendation is to proceed confidently, but with care. This concept is best summarized by Betsy Irvine: "Having been involved in service work for well over 20 years, I think that an important rule for people interested in service is one which follows the oft-quoted medical ethic, 'First, do no harm.' Too often, when people do service they figure (wrongly) that anything will do or that anything helps. That is simply not true. We would never allow someone to operate on us who did not have the experience, skill, and credentials to do so. Why should we expect less of work in communities? In some ways, doing service is like 'operating' in the community, and we need to approach it with the same respect, honesty, and care that we would our own life and community. We need to consider whether or not the service we do will have an adverse effect or an unexpected consequence. Such consideration requires a lot of thought and care, preparation, and reflection. Most importantly, it requires extensive input from those who are and will be affected by the work."

OK, so now that you're involved and are embarking upon your journey with community, we have four things we'd like for you to keep in mind.

Age should not be a barrier. You are never too young or too old to contribute to your community. We are reminded of the heartwarming but tragic story of Rachel Beckwith, who, in lieu of presents for her ninth birthday, asked instead for donations to the group *charity: water.* Rachel was motivated to collect donations after she learned that many children around the world don't live to age five because they lack access to safe drinking water. She set a modest goal of raising $300 and received donations of $220. Rachel was tragically killed in a car accident approximately one week after her birthday. When Rachel's story reached the national news, people around the world contributed to her charity. As of this writing, $1,265,824 has been raised for *charity: water* in Rachel's honor.

At the other end of life's spectrum, our hats are off to Charles Carroll, who volunteers twice a week in four-hour increments at Delray Medical Center in Florida. Charles is ninety-eight years old and has volunteered with a number of organizations and in a number of capacities throughout his life. Medical service has been Charles's passion, and his volunteer stints have included medical transport, checking in patients at clinics, and serving as the go-to person at the information desk of a hospital. Charles began his service to the Delray Medical Center five years ago, after he successfully recovered there from a heart attack. These two examples make it clear that no matter what age you are, it is possible to contribute to community.

Consider this example from our local community. The group Volunteers in Public Schools (VIPS) provides community support for public education and administers several volunteer programs that serve the educational needs of local children enrolled in public schools. VIPS hosts an annual awards ceremony in which it recognizes outstanding volunteers who work in service to public schools. The Crystal Apple Award is VIPS's highest award; it is given to a volunteer with at least 10 years of service to the school system. This past year, 7 outstanding volunteers were nominated by local public schools. Of these nominees, the fewest number of years of service to a school was 11; the most was 37. The average number of years of service for all nominees was 19. The 7 nominees had volunteered for a total of 135 years—a true testament to longevity in service to community.

The other thing to remember about working in community is not to underestimate anyone's contribution based on their age. Some may assume that particularly children and senior citizens may not contribute as much as others, but we have found this not to be the case. We have noticed that people who possess tender or great age are sometimes marginalized in community endeavors; their power is underestimated and undervalued, and we'd like to see that change. The U.S. government has capitalized on the collective strengths of senior citizen volunteers through SeniorCorps (see the appendix on volunteer organizations for more details). Please make sure that age is not a barrier in your travels in community.

Realize that your service experience may change over time. A lot can change over the course of your life, and it is logical to assume that your service to community will probably shift and change as your life does.

Consider the following experience of Mallory Trochesset. As she says: "My service experience has definitely evolved over time. When I first got involved in community service, I enjoyed the experience and felt good about giving back for a few hours every month; however, I never quite understood the social problem or root cause our service was even addressing. Now, as I am older and more socially aware, I challenge myself to stop and think about the needs of our community and how to best address them. One of the greatest examples I have of this new learning is when we hosted our annual Hunger and Homelessness Awareness Week events at the University of South Florida in 2010. I had been advising a group of college students on this event, yet had no idea about the homeless population in Tampa—and quickly learned that neither did our students hosting the event. Through the week-long series of programs, I learned that on any given night there are nearly 10,000 homeless men, women, and children in Tampa, but only 2,000 beds for them in the homeless shelters. Further, we had a former homeless woman come and speak at our Oxfam America Hunger Banquet, and she shared with us her journey into homelessness. Everyone has their assumptions about homeless persons—they're lazy, they're alcoholics, they're veterans, they're mentally challenged in some way—yet here was a woman with a master's degree and a family who desperately needed to get out of a physically abusive marriage and had nowhere to turn for help. To save her life and her children she went to the streets for nearly three months before she could get back on her feet. Now she is a leading advocate for homelessness issues and legislation in Tampa. It has not only changed my perspective as I engage with my community, but has inspired me to help college students also learn more about the organizations they serve, the projects they host, and the needs they meet."

We think it's important to start where you are with your current interests, skill sets, and available time. Though extended service produces greater impact and richer experiences, one day or episodic volunteer opportunities can be good starting points and can get you connected with others in your community. If you are in the process of choosing a career or considering a new one, volunteering can be an excellent way to experience and explore prospective careers, professions, and jobs, as well as to network.

Serving your community can also provide you with career and professional development opportunities, since you can learn and practice many of the same skill sets in a volunteer capacity that you would use in a professional capacity. You may even ultimately choose a career in the volunteer or nonprofit sector. Finally, you might consider national service as an option; this vast, well-organized network places volunteers for a set period of time—for example, one to two years—based on local and national needs. See the Appendix on volunteer organizations for details.

The communities in which you work and the issues in which you engage may change as your life changes geography-wise, time-wise, skill-wise, and interest-wise. Just remember that no matter your place in life, it is a place from which you can contribute to the community.

Your service doesn't have to be big to make an impact. We appreciate the passionate energy displayed by many volunteers who set out to change the world for the better. This is our goal as well. We've learned along the way, however, that a slow, steady pace tends to work better than a sprint.

The vast majority of tasks in service may seem mundane, but that doesn't make them any less important. We've noticed that many volunteers who express initial interest in engaging with community want to clean oil from a pelican or pluck people off roof tops after a hurricane. We call these experiences "MTV volunteer opportunities." We all like music, but none of us has been on MTV. Realize that being a volunteer rock star has more to do with showing up consistently and doing the little thing than swooping in and doing the dramatic thing. Planting the community garden is important and exciting; maintaining the garden over time may be less exciting than planting it but is even more important, because the weeding and watering over time eventually enable the plants to grow and the garden to be harvested.

We encourage you to be realistic in your expectations for positive community change. Professor Talmage Stanley reminds us that "woven into the fibers and sinews of every place is the basic reality of all human relationships: conflict." His statement is important to keep in mind when working with community. Change can be slow and difficult and may not seem transformative. We remind ourselves to keep moving forward on our path and not to be discouraged with slow progress. We remind ourselves that there is no need to reinvent the wheel. We have seen volunteer efforts wasted on creating new ways to do things instead of adding our capacity to existing structures that are already doing those things well. And we remind ourselves that there is no substitute for ordinary hard work that we undertake together over time, despite and even because of conflict.

Seek sustainability rather than short-term fixes. This concept is illustrated well by community leader Judy Bethly, who says: "Well-meaning, good-intentioned citizens arrive into poverty-stricken neighborhoods armed with paint brushes, buckets of paint, and smiles. Several hours later, not much has changed, except that a house is painted and the smiles of volunteers and the homeowner are forever captured on pictures.

What is wrong with this picture? Too many of these short-term, 'feel good' projects do not allow for systemic change. They are much appreciated —but nothing changes. In order to conduct meaningful community service, powerful change needs to occur within the dwellers of the community. Once the paint peels, the homeowner still lacks the self-sufficiency needed to paint her home, so she will again look for someone to rescue her from the situation or leave the house unpainted."

We have made a long-term commitment to serving the community because ultimately we want to address the policies and practices in our society that result in unfair and unequal access to goods and services. Thus, while all of us might perform service to our community that results in a short-term gain, such as painting a house, we also have our eyes set on long-term solutions that address an issue at its core.

As Judy continues, "Most poor communities possess institutions such as schools, churches, and small businesses. A more effective service strategy is to partner with the community's existing entities because their members know its history, the culture, and care about its continuance. We can work to enhance these institutions' strengths, always keenly listening to the dreams and vision of the group.

For example, school administrators complain about a lack of parental involvement. They suggest that parent/teacher conferences and school functions are not well attended. Our area is not recognized for its public transportation system, especially in the evening hours. An area business can partner with one of the churches in the community to provide funding to pay drivers to deliver parents and students to and from evening school events. Funding can also be used to pay the older siblings of students to babysit younger siblings while the parents are meeting. So that the funding is not just a 'feel good' intention, the business can match funds provided by the church and the school. In this instance, the business, the church, and the school have worked together to address a community need and can now continue to work together. More importantly, the partnership has empowered the participants with the knowledge to continue this work far into the future.

This short example makes it sound quite simple—it is, and it isn't. Trust needs to be established between all participating parties because in most poor communities, the fear of lack of resources creates a great deal of distrust. Hosting several 'get to know you' events along with meetings that allow everyone to expose any hidden agendas will help form the framework of long-term effective service that benefits an impoverished community."

In this example, Judy suggests that community constituencies work together to collectively provide their knowledge, expertise, and assets toward a solution for neighborhood revitalization or increased participation in public education. We applaud efforts like this because they involve everyone and provide a forum in which true conversations can take place about issues and conflicts, as well as practical ways to address them.

We also encourage all citizens to consider the features and structures of society that have led to the issue(s) we are trying to address through our service efforts. We all do a lot of work in the trenches to address immediate needs in conjunction with the issues we care about, but we also do big picture or broader thinking and actions toward trying to address those issues by ending the conditions that allowed them to be created in the first place.

For example, some of us serve as reading tutors to facilitate literacy for individual people. However, we also serve with organizations such as the Greater Baton Rouge Literacy Coalition, which spearheads efforts among several organizations and is executing a city-wide literacy plan. Some of us work with volunteer agencies that organize and coordinate literacy efforts throughout the state. Finally, some of us stay abreast of literacy issues on a broader scale through the National Coalition for Literacy or the International Reading Association, which provides information on policies that affect literacy (positively or negatively) and how to influence these policies as a citizen or group of citizens, in order to address literacy issues at a systemic level.

It is tackling issues both locally and globally ("glocally") that makes your efforts sustainable. In the example above, our ultimate goal is to eradicate illiteracy. This means that we might work with a person once a week in an effort to increase their literacy skills; call our congressperson once a month regarding funding for public education or Head Start, or to provide input on a bill before Congress involving literacy; meet with local or state leaders in literacy twice a year to coordinate and organize efforts; and contribute funds to local, state, national, or international groups on literacy issues once a year.

These types of efforts are transferrable to any issue of importance in which you choose to engage. Sustainable efforts over the long term are important because they address short term needs but also aim for a long-term solution.

We'd like to close this chapter by sharing some of our best experiences as a result of serving in our communities.

My agency, Volunteer Louisiana, funds AmeriCorps programs to do work in communities. Members commit to a year of service with a nonprofit, receive a very modest living stipend, and earn an Educational Award upon successful completion of their term of service. After Hurricane Katrina, we funded Trinity Christian Community in New Orleans (still do) as they did house gutting and rebuilding. The members worked on a home of an elderly woman whose grandson was living with her. He watched these passionate young people work to provide suitable housing for his grandmother. He became an AmeriCorps member the next year because he wanted to express his gratitude for these members who had given a year to help his family.

—Janet Pace

When I was at Yale Divinity School, the Yale chaplain at that time was William Sloan Coffin, one of the brightest stars of activism that our country has ever known. He talked to a group of us who were about to graduate from the Divinity School about the problems and possibilities of employment once we left the hallowed halls of Ivy League academia. He reminded us, when we complained about the lack of jobs, that we will NEVER be out of a job—oh yes, we might suffer from periods of unemployment or we might be employed in things unrelated to our study—but we will NEVER EVER be out of a job, because the job of the minister/theologian/activist is to make the world a better place, and there will always be room for that. Getting paid for it is pure lagniappe.

—Betsy Irvine

My passion is to help others in any way that I possibly can. I have seen my passion evolve from very young children to older seniors back to young, cancer-stricken patients, but the goal has always been the same—to lift others up. There are always some stories that forever lift your heart at the end of a very long day. I am a strong advocate for women's rights, and I always try to facilitate at least one civic engagement project every semester that will benefit young women who are struggling to succeed. This particular young lady that we shall call Lisa had two small children, no family to rely on, and a very abusive fiancé. One morning at 3 a.m. she called me and begged me to help her get into a shelter with her two children because she had had enough—two of her ribs were broken, she had a black eye, and her left foot had been crushed with a hammer by the drunk and disorderly fiancé. She had thirty-seven cents to her name. Things continually occurred to stop Lisa in her pursuit of a degree, but I never stopped telling her that good can triumph. With the help of members of my church and several good friends, we were able to help Lisa get through the next two years without huge incident. When she walked across the stage to receive her degree in nursing, the pride in her smile was mesmerizing. She is now a registered nurse in a local hospital (pediatrics specialty) and her two children are thriving in school. Had the battered women's project not come across my desk that semester, Lisa's life may have ended tragically. There is no paycheck big enough to ever reward any professional service-giver that can compete with the knowledge that you helped someone overcome chaos and adversity and find success.

—Phyllis Simpson

Before I began teaching in the LSU English department, I worked as a campus minister. I had the opportunity to accompany groups of college students on work trips to New York City where we worked in soup kitchens and homeless shelters. When I observed the impact of these experiences on the students, I knew that I wanted to help young people think about community issues from a variety of perspectives.

Soon after joining the English department, I met Jan Shoemaker and discovered service-learning. I had many questions and I wasn't sure how to integrate it with my coursework. When I shared my experiences with Jan, she said, "You're already doing service-learning; you just haven't been calling it that." She wouldn't take no for an answer.

When I began searching for a community partner, I immediately thought of the agencies and people with whom I had previously worked, including a local HIV/AIDS service agency where my clients were the homeless, prostitutes, and injecting drug users—the most disenfranchised, alienated, and overlooked people in society. Those people, many of whom suffered and died, taught me something significant about living with dignity in the most undignified circumstances.

I knew this would be controversial, but I wanted to shake the students out of their comfort zones. I wanted to challenge them to think about how their perspectives were influenced by their experiences and relationships, and I wanted to challenge their stereotypes. This eventually led to working with my present partner, Connections for Life (CFL), a nonprofit that provides services for indigent women who have been incarcerated, who struggle with substance abuse recovery, and who have survived poverty and abuse.

As a result of this partnership, my eyes were opened daily to the shocking realities of disenfranchised women in our culture. From the lack of basic services like health care to the injustice and sexism of the criminal justice system to the challenge of accessing education and finding employment— our culture makes it difficult beyond reason for women to improve their lives even when they have made the decision to do so.

I have numerous stories of how my life has been changed by those whom I have served. I'll briefly relate three:

Each semester, we invite a group of women from CFL to join us in my composition classroom for discussion and collaborative writing. One semester, the group included a young woman who had once wanted to be a geologist until her plans were interrupted by drug addiction and a prison sentence. She shared with us that she wanted to go back to school, but she was discouraged by the fact that many public colleges do not allow convicted felons to enroll. She said that she was so grateful to be there because she knew it was unlikely that she would ever have another opportunity to sit in a college classroom. CFL executive director Karen Stagg and I encouraged her to apply, and we worked with her to help her enroll at the University of New Orleans. I helped her with her admissions essay. Against the odds, she was accepted. She had a very successful first year and earned a B on her first college essay, and she gave me permission to share that essay with my composition students. She is now pursuing her dream, and it all started with that one classroom visit.

This past semester, a student enrolled in my poetry class had an interview for admission to medical school. During the interview, he was asked to articulate the difference between sympathy and pity. The student thought about it and answered the question by talking about a poem we had discussed in class called "Once in a While, a Protest Poem." He shared with the interviewer that the poem and his service experience with CFL had challenged him to think about the difference between sympathy and compassion and pity, and he fully answered the question. As he left the interview, one of the interviewers shook his hand, and said, "Remember that poem when you become a doctor."

Finally, the story of one personal service experience that changed my life. One Christmas when I was working with people affected by HIV/AIDS, I had organized a group of volunteers to put together gift boxes for clients. These were really just personal care items (shampoo, toothpaste, etc.) that we collected in shoe boxes, but we wrapped the packages and delivered them like good Christmas elves. At the end of the day on Christmas Eve, we had one package that still had to be delivered to a prostitute who lived in a "dangerous" part of town. I decided to deliver it myself. I drove to a small, dilapidated house in north Baton Rouge. Janice met me at the kitchen door and invited me into her home. She was so excited to receive that humble gift! With great excitement, she took me into the living room so we could put the package under the tree. The Christmas tree was really just a branch decorated with a homemade paper chain. It would have made Charlie Brown's sad tree look extravagant, but Janice was incredibly proud of it. "I finally have a present to put under it," she said, placing her decorated shoe box on the table next to the branch. She hugged me tightly and began to cry, repeating, "God bless you," over and over. She invited me to stay for dinner, but I declined since I had to get home to my family. She held my hand as she walked me to my car, still repeating, "You're an angel. God bless you." I drove home that night thinking about how sincerely she had extended a blessing to me. I had given her a shoe box of drug store samples—nothing really. She, who had nothing, had asked God to bless me, who was already so blessed! I learned more about what it means to serve in that half hour visit than in the rest of my life put together, and many times I have wished that I had stayed for dinner. A small thing that made a huge impact. On me.

—Sharon Williams Andrews

So that's it, our basic primer for getting involved in community. In summary, we can't recommend getting involved highly enough.

Each of us is rooted in our respective communities through long-term service. These roots have enabled us to build deep relationships with fantastic people we never would have met otherwise, and to contribute to building a just, fair, fun and welcoming community that we are honored to call home.

People who work together for the common good are a tribe. We are bound by our shared and different experiences, buoyed by the spaces we have opened up for true, honest dialogue and change, and forever linked through both simple and profound experiences involving things such as food and music, joy and sadness, learning and teaching, and creation and destruction.

This is our community.

This is your community.

Join us.

EPILOGUE

The LSU Community Playground Project is still making forward progress on our quest to provide children with safe, fun, accessible playgrounds. On our seventh try for funding, we received a $10,000 grant for the White Hills Elementary playground from the Cogburn Family Foundation, and we recently found out that Cogburn has decided to grant White Hills another $10,000 to supplement the swings we purchased with their initial grant. I am not sure who is more excited, me or White Hills principal Cheryl Lewis, who has also secured approximately $2,250 in donations for the new playground.

In conjunction with the leadership provided by Principal Patrice Hudson, the Buchanan Elementary School Parent Teacher Association and their community partner, the First Presbyterian Church of Baton Rouge, put together more than $26,000 and recently completed a new school playground.

We are actively working with approximately ten schools and organizations on designs, bid specifications, and/or funding for community playgrounds. Fireplug Cindy Murphy has been successful in securing several small grants for the Wildwood Elementary playground, but she is still searching for a large grant to complete the dream playground created by the children at Wildwood. Parkview Elementary fifth-graders are still playing in full view of a cemetery. Pre-kindergartners are still playing on three tree stumps. Westminster Elementary School contacted me a month ago; although they remain excited about the school-age playground we completed together in 2004, the pre-kindergarten students have precious little equipment to use, so we'll be collaborating again to transform the pre-kindergarteners' play space (which will not include a fire pole). We will never get past a phase I playground design at Brookstown Elementary because the school was recently closed.

I've had students enter my classroom who were touched by the playground project before reaching LSU. As a junior in high school, Josh Reaves built a playhouse at the McMains Children's Developmental Center for his Eagle Scout project. It was his initial spark that led to executive director Janet Ketcham launching a full-blown effort to upgrade the entire McMains playground. Josh and his team worked side by side with the LSU Community Playground Project to complete our respective parts of the playground. Two years later, Josh showed up in my playground design class; he went on to graduate with a degree in biological engineering and is now a successful practicing engineer.

Elizabeth Kissner, a student enrolled in my 2011 playground design class, told me that she grew up playing on the Villa del Rey playground, the one that Jeff and my high-achieving students toiled on in 2001. She remembers being a very excited nine-year-old on the day that the playground was completed. Deborah Gabriel, a veteran counselor at Villa del Rey, is also the mother of Mark Gabriel, a biological engineering graduate who did well in my class, volunteered on several playground builds during his undergraduate career, and is now a successful entrepreneur. Villa del Rey has become my first "three-peat" partnership. The LSU Community Playground Project is collaborating once again with the school, this time on their pre-kindergarten playground, from which all equipment was recently declared off-limits due to safety issues.

I still get to see Joe Howell through an annual LSU–Aramark–public school system partnership called Community Bound, in which incoming LSU freshmen work with LSU students, staff, and faculty to provide schoolyard clean up and beautification at numerous area public schools in a day of service facilitated by Aramark employees. Other than a broken foot sustained when the dunk tank chair he was sitting on collapsed unexpectedly, Joe is doing wonderfully. He is quick to say that he raised $500 for public schools during his stint in the dunk tank, which enabled employees of Aramark to take a crack at Joe for a nominal fee. As for me, I can still carry an eighty-pound bag of concrete when I have to, but it's harder to do at age forty-six than it was at age thirty-four.

Civic engagement is like an ocean that churns with challenge and success. I have body surfed these waves for more than a decade, and they still leave me enthused and nimble. I can't wait to learn and do more, and to revel in the souls of communities I have not yet met. For me, the two best sounds in the world are the ocean surf and the giggling of children; I hear both in the undertow of civic engagement, which firmly grounds me, heart and soul, in that place known as community.

Approximately five years ago, National Public Radio (NPR) commenced a series called "This I Believe." People wrote and submitted essays of five hundred words or less that described an artifact they fiercely believed in, and NPR screened the essays and asked the authors of the best essays to read them on the radio. The essays were fantastic and inspired me to write my own, which I dutifully submitted to NPR, and which NPR promptly rejected.

Undaunted by this "failure," I submitted the essay to the Baton Rouge newspaper, which runs a weekly column called "The Human Condition," containing anecdotes contributed by readers of the paper. My essay was published there. Shortly after it appeared, I spoke with Henry Landry, a lifelong Louisiana resident and member of my department's advisory council. "You know what?" he said to me, "After I read that essay, I knew it for sure. You're one of us." When a Cajun businessman from Thibodaux tells you "You're one of us," it is safe to say that you are. I consider his sentiment one of the highest compliments I've ever received.

I include the essay here because this book ends where it began, with a journey that continues to challenge and inspire me, a journey rooted in my home of south Louisiana and which includes communities in every corner of the globe.

I believe in Louisiana and the motto on her state flag, which is a succinct and inspiring road map for living. That motto is union, justice, confidence.

I was seduced by this place when I moved here eleven years ago. Louisiana is a place of characters, of people who live large in spirit and soul. It is a place where flowers bloom year-round, where water and land come together like a Monet masterpiece, a place where greens and blues are constant visual companions. Things flow through this place literally and figuratively, whether it is the water flowing south on the Mississippi, the oil flowing north to help power the rest of the country, the generous nature of natives, or the birds that stream through here by the millions in fall and spring.

I believe in Louisiana, not because it is perfect, but because of its big heart, conflicted soul, stunning beauty, and struggle to be better.

Things aren't fair here and they never have been; I suspect it's that way all over this country. Here in Louisiana, just as people live high-beamed and full frontal with their hearts, minds, and souls, social problems present themselves with equal vigor.

When confronted with such multifaceted issues, many people might shrink away. And yet, most people who I know in Louisiana don't. We work together to fight, scheme, and doggedly pursue the confluence of money, resolve, and community action to eliminate the "-isms" that result in Louisiana topping many of the bad lists and bottoming many of the good ones. This is true of the students I teach, the friends I have, and the communities with which I work. This is true of people all over the state, regardless of race, socioeconomic status, age, or hurricane impact status.

Life in Louisiana has taught me that it's better to have your eyes and heart wide open so that you can see, think, and do. Life in Louisiana has taught me that success is not about the ultimate outcome of a journey or struggle, it's about navigating the process. And it's taught me that sea change can and does occur through ordinary human effort and not extraordinary superhuman accomplishment.

I have come to the conclusion that I would rather struggle with an issue in full-blown Technicolor than to watch on the sidelines and intellectualize. And that is the essence of Louisiana—it is a dynamic, imperfect roil of success and failure, triumph and despair. I cannot think of another place I'd rather be, or another path I'd rather take.

APPENDIX 1

Information on Playground Safety

Accidents on playgrounds are the second most frequent reason that children visit the emergency room every year in the United States, with an estimated 200,000 visits per year (bike accidents are the first at 300,000 annual visits). Approximately fifteen children die every year on playgrounds. There are numerous sources of information on playground safety in the public domain, so rather than making this appendix a comprehensive guide to playground safety (which could be a book in itself), I will provide links to this information and will discuss the safety issues I tend to see and/or worry about the most in my travels around playgrounds.

Excellent Links about Playground Safety.

To start learning more about playground safety, I'd begin with the **National Program for Playground Safety** at www.uni.edu/playground/. Information is geared toward the public and is organized into different types of playground considerations depending on the venue, including elementary schools, childcare centers, residential homes, and youth organizations. Information is also available regarding playground safety standards, plans and research, safety training, products, and fundraising for a playground. There is also a section specifically geared toward children so that they can be aware of safety issues: www.uni.edu/playground/kids/main.htm. If you thoroughly read the information on this website, you will have an excellent understanding of playground safety.

If you need the expertise of a person who has a comprehensive knowledge of playground safety, you should work with a **certified playground safety inspector,** or CPSI. A CPSI is proficient with all playground safety recommendations and guidelines and has taken and passed a national exam on playground safety. CPSIs can perform playground safety audits and/or inspections for planned or existing playgrounds; they can also help you develop a comprehensive safety plan for your playground. There is a national registry of CPSIs: ipv.nrpa.org/cpsi_registry/default.aspx. If you go to this registry and put in your ZIP code or your state, available CPSIs and their contact information will be displayed. The **National Recreation and Park Association** (NRPA) has a link to information about playground safety at www.nrpa.org/playgroundsafety/. The site contains media releases involving playground safety and includes information on how to become a CPSI. You can also download a copy of "The Dirty Dozen" for your personal use; this short pamphlet contains excellent information on the twelve most important things to watch out for regarding playground safety.

Playground safety guidelines and standards are available from a number of sources. The **Consumer Product Safety Commission** (CPSC) publishes the "Handbook for Public Playground Safety," which is available at www .cpsc.gov/cpscpub/pubs/325.pdf and which explains technical information on playground safety standards, guidelines, and recommendations in a straightforward manner. The handbook covers three age groups: toddlers (6–23 months), preschool-age children (ages 2–5) and school-age children (ages 5–12). The **American Society for Testing and Materials** (ASTM) has a number of playground safety standards for purchase that are written in technical language. These standards are typically used by CPSIs and other professionals in playground design and manufacturing. You can search the ASTM site (www.astm.org) with the keyword "playground" to get a list of available standards for purchase.

Head Start Body Start: The National Center for Physical Development and Outdoor Play contains information and resources geared toward playgrounds for younger children (5 years of age and younger, with a focus on children ages 3–5). The section on their site entitled "Creating High Quality Outdoor Play Spaces" (www.aahperd.org/headstartbodystart/playspace/tools-and-resources.cfm) contains excellent information about items to include in a play space, as well as recommended publications on outdoor play spaces. The Play Space Assessment Survey on this webpage is an excellent rubric for examining a play space intended for 3–5 year olds and for determining what to add (or subtract) to enhance a playground for children in this age range.

As a person who has spent a lot of time on playgrounds, as well as someone who is a CPSI, my concerns are based on theory and practice. I will state at the outset that this is my personal list of concerns about playground safety; as I tell my students, when n = 1 (n being the number of points in your data set, and one meaning me and me only), you should interpret with care. So please take this for what it is: an informed opinion, but an opinion nonetheless. If you ask a different expert, you will probably get a somewhat different set of concerns. My best advice is to collect multiple opinions in order to choose the best course of action for your situation. If you want to become an advocate for playground safety, I cannot recommend CPSI training highly enough. The following paragraphs contain my five biggest concerns (in bold) about playground safety.

Experts estimate that 84 percent of all serious playground accidents can be eliminated with two things: proper maintenance of playgrounds (40 percent) and adult supervision (44 percent). In my opinion, the most important part of playground maintenance involves **playground safety surfacing**. Seventy-nine percent of all playground accidents that send kids to the emergency room occur because children fall from equipment. When they fall, children should land on a soft, shock-absorbing material. There are a number of playground safety surfacing materials that effectively break falls; it is critical to keep these materials maintained at the proper depth under and around play equipment. *Dirt and grass are not acceptable surfaces!* The CPSC "Handbook for Public Playground Safety" has detailed information regarding playground safety surfacing.

Lack of playground safety surfacing is an especially big issue on backyard playgrounds. Although more accidents occur on public playgrounds than on backyard playgrounds, accidents on backyard playgrounds account for more than half of all annual playground fatalities. All playgrounds with elevated equipment must have playground safety surfacing in order to be safe! Although surfacing will probably cost as much as the backyard playground equipment, it is absolutely critical to the safety of the children who will use the equipment. Make sure that your home playground has the proper use zone (the area under and around your play equipment in which children will land if they fall), a proper playground safety surfacing material that is contained within the use zone, and the proper depth of surfacing.

In terms of adult supervision, there are several issues that merit attention.

What not to wear on playgrounds. Children can become entangled while playing and can actually be strangled as a result. Thus, they should not wear things that tend to become entangled, including clothing with drawstrings (hood or neck drawstrings especially), jewelry (especially necklaces), scarves, and backpacks. I am a huge proponent of wearing bicycle helmets while riding a bicycle, but children should never wear a bicycle helmet on a playground! Helmets can result in children's heads becoming entrapped in openings that they would pass through easily without a helmet, causing a strangulation risk.

Watch for shade. One in five Americans will develop skin cancer sometime during their lives. I encourage the liberal use of sunscreen for anyone on the playground! Shade should also be a consideration on the playgrounds themselves: watch out for non-coated metal in the sun, for example, on slides and monkey bars. Temperatures on sun-exposed metal can reach more than 250 degrees Fahrenheit on playgrounds, especially during the summer, and can cause first-, second-, and even third-degree burns if children come into contact with these hot surfaces. Shade structures have gotten very popular on playgrounds recently to address these concerns, with entire playgrounds being placed under large "shade tents." These tents are expensive; remember that well-placed trees are an aesthetic, sustainable, and cheaper way to provide shade on playgrounds. Be sure to choose trees without exposed roots, which are tripping hazards.

Do not let little kids play on equipment intended for big kids. All public playgrounds must clearly mark which equipment is intended for preschool-age children (2–5 years old) and which is intended for school-age children (5–12 years old). Almost every time I visit a public playground, I watch adult caregivers allowing or even encouraging toddlers or preschool-age children to play on equipment intended for school-age children. Please don't! Playground equipment has been carefully designed to meet the developmental needs of children based on age; placing children on equipment beyond their developmental age greatly increases their chances of being hurt.

Remember the choking game. Recently, teenagers (primarily) have been hanging rope from elevated playground equipment and using this rope to play the "choking game," in which they deliberately hang themselves in order to experience a "high" that occurs just before passing out. The idea is that a group of friends will rescue each other from being strangled to death, but this "game" has—unsurprisingly—resulted in deaths. If you see a hanging rope (one that is not securely attached to the equipment and the ground or to the equipment on both ends), you should contact the playground staff to have it removed immediately, or remove it yourself. Some public-recreation facilities do daily checks to ensure that all hanging ropes are removed from their playgrounds.

Playground safety is a critically important component of any playground, and all playgrounds—whether public, backyard, church, day-care center, Head Start center, and so on—should have a safety plan and safety features in place. I encourage you to have conversations about playground safety with the staff of organizations who operate playgrounds in order to ensure the safety of your community's children.

If you find that you need the assistance of a playground safety professional, for example, a CPSI or playground manufacturing representative, proceed with caution. Most professionals have great integrity, are excited to share their knowledge with you, and are as passionate about children's safety as I am. A CPSI can perform a playground safety audit and can help you to develop a comprehensive safety plan (these are paid services). There are about two hundred reputable playground manufacturing companies in the United States; most have representatives that serve local or regional communities. These representatives can help you to design a playground using the components manufactured by the national company, or they can provide you with several possible designs based on the activities you are interested in seeing on a playground. These services are generally free, as the representative will make money based on the equipment you actually purchase.

I encourage you to compare costs, since some CPSIs may charge more than others and everyone has a justification for what they charge. Cost differences are especially marked with playground designs that are bid on by different playground manufacturing company representatives. Play equipment is expensive, but even on a small playground, some representatives will charge more than double what others do for the exact same thing! **Shop around.** If someone is representing a playground manufacturing company, it's in their best interest to sell you their products; you need to keep that in mind. Also keep in mind that most representatives can offer a decent discount (for example, 25 percent) from the price listed online or in the playground company's manufacturing catalog.

The final thing to remember is to not be frightened into spending lots of money. I've fielded calls from people in charge of playgrounds who are ready to spend big bucks (for example, $50,000) to bring their playgrounds into compliance with safety recommendations when a modest investment (say, $3,000) would suffice. Though rare, some sales reps sell a lot of equipment based on fear. It makes sense that many playground manufacturing companies have sales representatives who are also CPSIs (or have them on staff); because play equipment is their livelihood, it makes sense for these companies to be proficient with playground safety. Be careful of conflating playground safety with the purchasing of equipment. You may want to hire an independent CPSI to assist you with the safety needs of a playground, and/or work with a number of playground manufacturing representatives to develop the design you like best that is also the most economical.

APPENDIX 2

Volunteer Organizations

If you are not sure where to start regarding volunteer opportunities, have a look at the following information, which is presented in order of scale from local to global.

Locally

Many service organizations register with a local entity that tracks and provides information to these organizations. Check with your local mayor's office; many have an Office of Civic Engagement and Volunteer Service or an Office of Community Engagement. You might also check with your local universities if you have them, because most universities have established volunteer programs and/or service-learning offices to engage students in their local communities through service and learning.

State-wide

Check with your state's governor's office. Many have Offices of Volunteerism, or of Community Initiatives, etc. These offices can connect you to volunteer opportunities throughout your state, or in particular regions of your state.

Nationally

Corporation for National and Community Service (CNCS). www.national service.gov/. This federal agency connects volunteers and volunteer organizations. CNCS has three national programs: Senior Corps, AmeriCorps, and Learn and Serve America. SeniorCorps connects people 55 and older with addressing community needs. AmeriCorps has three separate programs geared toward people generally 18–24 years of age, including AmeriCorps State and National, AmeriCorps VISTA (Volunteers to Service in Americas), and AmeriCorps NCCC (National Civilian Community Corps). Participants in these programs receive living expenses in exchange for full-time volunteering within a community. Learn and Serve America provides support to schools (both K–12 and higher education) for service-learning, a method in which students master academic course content through service to the community. Two websites within CNCS may be helpful:

- Volunteeringinamerica.gov/. Includes information on volunteering on a national basis and also provides detailed information about volunteering in each state.
- www.serve.gov/. National online resource in which you can find local service activities by entering your ZIP code and key words describing your interests.

Internationally

Points of Light Institute. www.pointsoflight.org/. This organization runs three major units: the HandsOn Network, AmeriCorps Alums, and Generation On. The HandsOn Network mobilizes volunteers through action centers throughout the world (primarily in the United States). AmeriCorps Alums provides services for people who have previously served as AmeriCorps volunteers. Generation On facilitates the involvement of youth in volunteer service throughout the world.

idealist.org. An organization committed to all people living free, dignified lives by connecting resources, organizations, and people. Their site contains worldwide volunteer opportunities, current information about academic and employment opportunities, and internships in the nonprofit sector.

NOTE ON SOURCES

For further information regarding some of the concepts and events discussed in the text, see the following sources:

Chapter 1

The *Brown v. Board of Education* Supreme Court decision in 1954 produced a sea change in public education in the United States. The basic concept brought forth by this decision—that separate but equal is not equal—is a morally correct, straightforward idea that has driven my work with the LSU Community Playground Project. My experiences in this context have led me to believe that school desegregation is a far more complicated process than one might initially suspect, and that it is a force still at work today. I recommend the following two books for those wanting to learn more about *Brown v. Board of Education:* Richard Kluger, *Simple Justice: The History of* Brown v. Board of Education *and Black America's Struggle for Equality* (New York: Vintage, 1994), and James T. Patterson, *Brown v. Board of Education: A Civil Rights Milestone and Its Troubled Legacy* (New York: Oxford University Press, 2002).

Page 8: The Consumer Product Safety Commission publishes the Handbook for Public Playground Safety, which can be viewed online at www.cpsc.gov/cpscpub/pubs/325.pdf. This publication, written in an accessible style, is updated periodically and contains information on playground injury statistics, as well as comprehensive information on playground safety recommendations.

Page 14: For more information on the settlement of the desegregation lawsuit in Baton Rouge, listen to a National Public Radio story aired on Morning Edition, August 15, 2003: www.npr.org/player/v2/mediaPlayer.html?action=1&t=1&islist=false&id=13 97079&m=1397080.

Chapter 2

Page 32: Paul Loeb is an activist, author, and speaker with an important message about getting involved in civic society. He has a regularly updated website, www.paulloeb .org, and he also blogs at the Huffington Post, www.huffingtonpost.com/paul-loeb. I recommend his book, *Soul of a Citizen: Living with Conviction in Challenging Times*, 2nd ed. (New York: St. Martin's Griffin, 2010).

Page 34: KaBOOM! is a nonprofit organization dedicated to building a playground within walking distance of every child in the United States. Their website can be found at kaboom.org/. It contains good information on building playgrounds, getting them funded, and strategies for increasing play time and activities in the daily lives of children.

Chapter 3

Page 43: Janet Eyler is Professor of the Practice of Education at Vanderbilt University and a national pioneer for service-learning in higher education. Her quote comes from a plenary address that she delivered at the Gulf South Summit at Belmont University in Nashville, Tenn., March 13–15, 2008. Another great quote from the same address is: "Fear makes us stupid." Dr. Eyler is best known for the 1999 book she coauthored with Dwight E. Giles Jr., *Where's the Learning in Service-Learning?* (San Francisco: Jossey-Bass, 1999). This outstanding book is on almost every library shelf in service-learning offices across the United States, including LSU's.

Page 45: The actual population of Renaissance Village was difficult to pinpoint, as the population was constantly in flux. The numbers reported here are based on conversations that the YK Coalition had with FEMA. I cite them in my article, "Inside the Eye: Playground Design in a Hurricane-Induced Trailer Park City." *Resource Magazine* 14(3) (2007): 9–10.

Page 49: A technical report on the susceptibility of electrode blowout in cochlear implants can be found at www.access-board.gov/research/play-slides/report.htm. Head entrapments are generally openings between 3.5" and 9" To be sure if an opening is in fact a head entrapment, a test is conducted using standard probes as described in ASTM F1487-11, "Standard Consumer Safety Performance Specification for Playground Equipment for Public Use" (available for purchase at www.astm.org/Standards/F1487.htm). This test should be conducted by a certified playground safety inspector. The Louisiana Office of the State Fire Marshal publishes the code that must be followed in the construction of artifacts such as residential and commercial buildings. This report, which states that openings in fences and gates must not allow a four-inch sphere to pass through them, can be found at sfm.dps.louisiana.gov/doc/ms-a/ms-alr_rules.pdf.

Chapter 4

Page 80: The FBI publishes the uniform crime report on an annual basis, as well as preliminary semiannual uniform crime reports. Annual reports can be viewed at www.fbi.gov/about-us/cjis/ucr/crime-in-the-u.s. Information from these reports was used by the local news station WAFB to report the murder rate of the city of Baton Rouge, www.wafb.com/story/14831241/baton-rouge-has-7th-highest-murder-rate-in-nation. Baton Rouge crime statistics can be viewed at brgov.com/dept/brpd/csr.

Chapter 5

Page 91: In his book *The Tipping Point* (New York: Back Bay Books, 2002), author Malcolm Gladwell has an excellent discussion of what he has dubbed "the law of 150" on pages 177–181.

Page 93: The Americans with Disabilities Act of 1990 (and subsequent amendments) can be read at www.ada.gov/pubs/ada.htm. The Architectural Barriers Act of 1968 (with amendments) also has excellent information on accessibility requirements, www.fs.fed.us/recreation/programs/accessibility/Architectural_Barriers.htm. The Architectural and Transportation Barriers Compliance Board, also known as the Access Board, has published the most updated guidelines and standards as they relate to accessibility at www.access-board.gov/ada/. For additional information regarding the ADA as it applies to playground design, consult the Consumer Product Safety Commission's Handbook for Public Playground Safety and the ADA accessibility guidelines for play areas (www.access-board.gov/play/finalrule.htm). For more technical, design-focused information, see ASTM standards F1487-11 and F1951-09b, "Standard Specification for Determination of Accessibility of Surface Systems Under and Around Playground Equipment," online at www.astm.org/Standards/F1951.htm).

Page 95: A Reading Friend is a tutor trained by a Baton Rouge–based nonprofit organization called Volunteers in Public Schools to work one-on-one with a child enrolled in kindergarten, first, second, or third grade who is reading below grade level. Reading Friends have made a tremendous impact in enabling this targeted group of students to achieve grade-level proficiency in reading. VIPS' website is vips.ebrschools.org. I am a proud advisory board member of this outstanding organization.

Page 100: Ken Reardon is Professor and Director of Graduate Studies in City and Regional Planning at the University of Memphis. He told the story about "fire, aim, ready" during a presentation at the Louisiana Campus Compact Fall Scholars Day on November 7, 2007.

Page 101: Donna Brazile uttered these statements during a keynote presentation at the Listening to Louisiana Women Symposium held in Baton Rouge on May 25, 2011. The candidate she campaigned for at age nine was elected, and the playground promised by the politician was built. She secured funds to rebuild this very same playground after Hurricane Katrina destroyed it in 2005. I recommend her autobiography, *Cooking with Grease: Stirring the Pots in American Politics (New York: Simon and Schuster, 2005)*.

Chapter 6

Page 119: ECERS-R is the Early Childhood Environment Rating Scale; it is a quality assessment instrument for various aspects of pre-kindergarten, kindergarten, and child-care classrooms, and includes guidelines on playgrounds.

Page 124: Professor Lesia Crumpton-Young teaches industrial engineering at the University of Central Florida. She shared the Texas version of a no during a presentation at the Leadership Development Conference hosted by the Women in Engineering Leadership Institute at Cocoa Beach, Fla., April 28 –May 1, 2005.

Chapter 7

Pages 139 and 145. Talmage Stanley made these insightful statements during his plenary talk entitled "Places Your GPS Can't Take You" at the Gulf South Summit in Roanoke, Va., on March 3, 2011.

Page 141: For more information about Rachel Beckwith and charity: water, see www.mycharitywater.org/p/campaign?campaign_id=16396. For more information about Charles Carroll, see www.palmbeachpost.com/community-post/at-98-former-patient-is-delray-medical-centers-1627194.html.

Page 142: The nominees for the 2011 Crystal Apple Award through Volunteers in Public Schools were Jason Jones, Pastor Alfred Moore III, Marilyn Shalley-Damburg, Buddy Tucker, Caroline Whicker, Larry Wilkinson, and Judy Young. Jason Jones received the Crystal Apple Award.

Page 147: The website for the National Coalition for Literacy or the International Reading Association is www.national-coalition-literacy.org.

ACKNOWLEDGMENTS

First and foremost, I acknowledge all the community partners and community members with whom I have had the privilege of collaborating to design and build playgrounds. Thanks especially to all the former and current students, faculty, and administration in the East Baton Rouge Parish Public School System and at Louisiana State University. I commend the company Aramark, whose corporate culture sets a model in terms of community engagement. The playground project would never work without the buy-in and hard work of the people affiliated with these organizations. I also acknowledge the thousands of people and organizations who have contributed time, money, ideas, and inspiration.

People who have enabled the LSU Community Playground Project to thrive include Pat Duhon, Catherine Fletcher, Scot Givens, Ken Koonce, Belinda Martinez, Robert Martinez, Kenny Kohler, Treynor McAdams, Adam Pfeiffer, Julie Smith, Dan Thomas, and Lalit Verma. The organizational structure of this program does not fit easily into established university policies and procedures and has required tremendous time input from a number of people to make it work, including Jim Bates, Danielle Bayham, Lisa Geddes Capone, Gina Dugas, Donna Elisar, Charlotte Fruge, Russell Greer, Jeff Hale, David Hardy, Ping Li, Jeff McClain, Tom McClure, Eric Monday, Theresa Russo, Rhonda Shepard, and Angela Singleton. Two additional staunch supporters are Richard "Dick" Bengtson and Joe Howell. Dick has set the gold standard on the LSU campus of what it means to be committed to student success; he is to the LSU campus what Joe Howell is to our local public schools. When I think about what it means to be a great man, I think of two half-horsepower guys standing shoulder to shoulder: Joe and Dick.

The culture of service-learning on the LSU campus has also been a critical ingredient to the success of this program. I stand on the shoulders of local pioneers who built service-learning and community engagement initiatives before me and/or who practiced in the trench with me, especially Cecile Guin, Connie Hicks, Barrett Kennedy, Renee Boutte Myer, Deborah Normand, Carol O'Neil, Robert Perlis, Jan Shoemaker, George Stanley, Larry Rouse, Maud Walsh, and Colonel Harold Webb.

To date, I've had the privilege of instructing approximately a thousand students during my career. Although it is impossible to acknowledge every student I've ever taught by name on these pages, I do acknowledge every single student I've ever had. The following current and former students are those who shared greatly of their time and immense talents to help build the LSU Community Playground Project from the ground up. Thank y'all for everything, and for the inspiration: Julianne Forman Audiffred, Megan Barnum, Jacob Beckham, Sandeep Bhale, Clayton Birkett, T. Kyle Bridges, John Casey, Patrick Coco, Nick Coleman, Jennifer Craig, Tessa Byrne Craig, Andrea Albright Crawford, Tony Daigle, Cody Darnell, Kristen Galloway, Sarah De Leo, Leah Moore Eisenstadt, Jason El Koubi, W. Chandler Emery, Stuart Feilden, Jacob Fusilier, Bilal Ghosn, Matt Gravens, Xinmei Guo, Komi Hassan, Carla Haslauer, Emily Hodges, Melinda Hunter, Jennifer Istre, Jackie Jones Edward, Andrew Keller, Brandon Kilbourne, Alicia Abadie Modenbach, Brooke Morris, Sean Nolan, Czarina Patolilic, Sajid Qadri, Malcolm Richard, Tel Rouse, Katie Rousseau, Rebecca Canfield Schramm, Jeremy Theriot, Michelle O'Brien Urbina, Nicole Walker, Alexandra Williams, Lakiesha Claude Williams, Sarah Williams, and N. Jeaux Zerkus.

I am lucky enough to have my own group of "the ladies," my soul sisters in community engagement. Sharon Williams Andrews, Christy Kayser

Arrazattee, Judy Bethly, Roxanne Dill, Lynn Hathaway, Saundra McGuire, Deborah Normand, Carol O'Neil, Peggy Reily, Jean Rohloff, Cindy Seghers, Jan Shoemaker, and Karen Stagg—all y'all are my slice of heaven. Yoga instructor Carmen Board, oriental medical doctor and acupuncturist Ching Guo, and social worker Stella Brown have had a profoundly positive impact on my life. I have benefited greatly from their collective wisdom and talent, and I consider them honorary ladies as well.

I graduated from high school twenty-seven years ago. That kind of time creates a perspective that distills defining moments and makes clear influential teachers. I had two influential teachers. One was Mrs. Jeanne Dinwoodie, who taught math and the discipline of deep study in equal measure. While I struggled with both in high school (particularly the latter), I learned enough from Mrs. Dinwoodie to make every college math class I ever took a breeze. Since math is a major underpinning of engineering, I know that Jeanne Dinwoodie had a lot to do with my success in college and, by extension, my career thereafter. My second influential teacher was Mr. Todd Evans. As a senior, I opted out of honors English because I wanted to take creative writing, which was not part of the honors curriculum (I sure hope someone has changed that policy since then). Mr. Evans was my creative writing teacher, and he was wonderful and inspiring. As a budding writer, I always had the stolid support of my parents, who read and loved everything I wrote from age five onward. As incredibly important as that support was, as a senior, I wasn't sure if anyone beyond my parents thought my writing was any good. Mr. Evans provided that spark of confidence while also teaching me a lot about style and practice, including the importance of writing every day. When I informed him that I was heading to college to study engineering, he was almost appalled. "I really think you could make it as a professional writer," he told me. I never forgot his sentiments, and I'm happy to report all these years later that writing is the most often used skill of this engineer. Both these teachers provided me with roots and wings; it is these things I try to instill in my students today.

Although Mr. Evans nurtured my aspirations as a writer, it was Mr. Richard "Dick" DeLong who came at my writing with what initially felt like an axe, but what in actuality was the laser-sharp critical intensity that taught me that writing could be a transformative force for action. I worked for two years as a writer and then one year as editor for my college's quarterly engineering magazine, which was produced entirely by students. No one taught me more about writing than Dick DeLong, veteran journalist and faculty advisor of this publication. Dick spent many hours with me to help hone my writing skills; he was never paid a dime for his post as voluntary advisor. I use what he taught me every day. I also use his unselfish example as my inspiration to provide the same thoughtful but critical editing for my own students.

I am blessed with absolutely awesome family, friends, and colleagues (artificial separations to be sure, because I consider them all part of my family). I am lucky to be part of three clans—Hathaway, Lima, and Rogers—and I acknowledge every member of each clan. The Hathaways are the model of seeing what needs to be to be done and then doing it right. The Limas taught me that adversity is a normal part of life and that the best way to deal with it is to gut through it. From the Rogerses, I learned about the importance of integrity and sticking to it. My brother John is no holds barred the best brother anyone could ever ask for. My mother, Kathleen Rogers, and father, John Lima Sr., are very different people, yet each is a trailblazer in their own ways, and each instilled in me the importance of standing up for fairness and equality. I could not have asked for better parents. My aunts Shirley Ferreira, Marthamarie Fuller, and Nancy Leaver have taught me courage, generosity, and grace, while Sharon Ferreira, Julie Johnson, Elizabeth Lima, Sarah Lima, and Chris Rogers have been exemplars of playfulness and sincerity. My grandmother Florence Rogers was named a woman of the year for her extensive, long-term volunteer work in New Bedford, MA. I deeply thank my friends and colleagues for their steadfast support and care: Dorin Boldor, Ann Christy, Kristi Davis, Sherry Desselle, Carol Friedland, M. Betsy Garrison, Diana Glawe, Connie Kuns, Lisa Launey, Linda Lee, Elaine Maccio,

W. Todd Monroe, Carol Lee Moore, Leslie Morreale, Sarah Myers, Sue Nokes, the entire Ropers-Huilman clan, Cristina Sabliov, and Emily Toth.

As I look back over my life, I know that people have been there for me during absolutely critical times; those I've not already mentioned include Toni Tumpek Doty, Tom and Blanche Judd, Jan Mackichan, Margaret Pepe, Beth Pratt, Mary Sansalone, and Sudhir Sastry.

Words cannot describe what a wonderful partner Lynn Hathaway is, or the depth of love I have for her. Lynn makes me feel like I am the permanent "king of the tire." She listened to me chatter every day about this book for fourteen months with full attention and without complaint. Every day. If that's not an expression of true love, I'm not sure what is. Lynn has volunteered on more playground builds than anyone. I am a very lucky woman.

In terms of this book, I'd like to thank MaryKatherine Callaway, who suggested writing it in the first place. I don't think it would have ever occurred to me to write this book if she hadn't suggested it. At the moment of this writing, this book feels like the best thing I've ever done professionally, so thank you, MaryKatherine! If you've been writing for a long time, you are well aware of the value of a good editor (as well as the dearth of truly outstanding editors). I was blessed with Alisa Plant, whose comments were always insightful and timely, and whose suggestions elevated the quality of the manuscript immensely. Alisa's support from day one of this process always made me feel like I had a personal cheerleader.

Writing this book required me to hole up about once a week in five-hour blocks of time for the fourteen months it took to create the manuscript. I had to delegate some of the work I would normally have done myself in order to make time to write. Christy Arrazattee was the recipient of the majority of tasks I delegated; and because of her ability to get a lot done and done well, Christy is a big part of the reason that I finished this book as fast as I did. I am eternally grateful to her for her work ethic and her patience.

Nicole Walker took the lead on fact checking for the book, and Victoria Hauth, Monica Montenegro, Whitney Mosel, and Matt Viator also assisted in this regard. Nicole is also a talented photographer, and several of her photographs grace these pages. Nicole and Bijeet Mukherjee also provided technical support with electronic image preparation.

Several readers pored over early drafts. Debbie Normand read every word I wrote early and eagerly; her comments were immensely helpful and 100 percent on target. Others who contributed their editing excellence include Lynn Hathaway, Linda Lee, Kathleen Rogers, Jan Shoemaker, and Dorothy Thrasher. Tracy Morris read the technical parts of the book to provide an engineer's perspective.

The title of this book has gone through more drafts than a herring gull does plumage changes in going from juvenile to adult (trust me, that's a lot). Many kind souls contributed to its myriad drafts, including Kristi Davis, Lynn Hathaway, Alisa Plant, Kathleen Rogers, and Dorothy and Ted Thrasher.

Finally, I acknowledge my community, that roiling ball of people, places, and other inhabitants that moor us together in a common trench, in which we all doggedly work together to positively impact the common good. There are Lamar and Keke in Coates Hall, Sandy, Brandon, and Sylvia in the Dairy Store, Janice in the South Stadium Drive traffic booth, and Maggi's book club in Johnston Hall. Martha, Joan, Billie Jean, and Jane, who race walk with me every Thursday morning, and Linda B., who runs with me every Friday morning. There are Celeste, Linda M., and Cissee in my yoga class, and Jean, Murray, C. J., and Mr. Willy in my neighborhood. There's also Albert the mailman, and Stephanie and her crew serving awesome soul food at Zeeland Street Market. We and countless others undergird and support each other in large ways and in small, in ways we can see and in ways that we can't. Ultimately, we all are truly connected.

INDEX

Abadie, Robelynn, 45

Agrestics, 7–8, 10–12, 15, 38, 86, 128

American Association of Higher Education (AAHE), 108

American Society for Engineering Education (ASEE), 108

American Society for Testing and Materials (ASTM), 160, 171–172

Americans with Disabilities Act of 1990 (ADA), 93–94, 172

AmeriCorps, 148, 167,

Andrews, Sharon Williams, 132, 152

Angels, 32

Architectural Barriers Act, 93, 172

Arrazattee, Christy Kayser, 132

Assumptions: in engineering, 47, 91; harmful, 46–51, 54, 92, 94, 143

Barnum, Megan, 82

Baton Rouge Area Foundation (BRAF), 62

Baton Rouge Recreation and Parks Department, 46

Baton Rouge Rotary Club, 44

Beckwith, Rachel, 141, 173

Beechwood Elementary School, 1–9, 11–17, 39, 56, 83

Bethly, Judy, 132, 145

Board, Carmen, 31, 131

Bordelon, Christa, 52

Boys Hope Girls Hope, 101

Brazile, Donna, 101, 172

Brock, Kandiest, 65, 71, 74, 76, 86

Brookstown Elementary School, 71, 155

Brown v. Board of Education, 169

Brown v. Board of Education: A Civil Rights Milestone and Its Troubled Legacy, 169

Brusly Elementary School, 34–35, 90, 97, 124

Buchanan Elementary School, 154

Buchanan Elementary School Parent Teacher Association, 154

Carnahan, Carolyn, 133

Carroll, Charles, 141, 173

Carter, Tiffany, 67

Catalysts, The, 30

Cedarcrest Southmoor Elementary School, 71

Center for Community Engagement, Learning, and Leadership (CCELL), 116

Certified Playground Safety Inspector (CPSI), 16, 57, 160–161, 164–165, 171

Chaos theory, 103–104

Checklist Manifesto, The, 120

Choking game, The, 163

Christmas Story, A, 122–123

Cochlear implants, 49–51, 171

Coffin, William Sloan, 148

Cogburn Family Foundation, 154

Community: definition of, 88; foot soldiers, 31; soul of the (*see* Soul of the Community)

Connections for Life (CFL), 150–151

Consumer Product Safety Commission (CPSC), 160, 162, 169, 172

Cornell University, 2, 112

Corporation for National and Community Service, 62, 167

Court Appointed Special Advocates (CASA), 154

Crestworth Elementary School, 69, 71

Crumpton-Young, Lesia, 124, 173

Crystal Apple Award, 142, 173

Cutie Patootie Center, 57

Daigle, Blythe, 133

Daigle, Tony, 67, 82, 84–86

de Toqueville, Alexis, 140

Desanti, Roger, 95

Dr. Seuss, 107

Duke, Jenola, 133

Early Childhood Environment Rating Scale (ECERS-R), 119, 173

East Baton Rouge Master Gardeners Association , 34, 101

East, Laura, 3, 9

Edison, Thomas Alva, 107

Elisar, Donna, 66, 71

Engineered wood fiber, x, 56, 82, 83

Engineering, Biological & Agricultural, ix

Engineering, Biological, ix, 15, 48

Engineering design, 3, 26, 47, 53, 54, 111–112

Etier, Brian, 18

Eyler, Janet, 43, 127, 170

Facilitators, The , 26

Failure: in engineering, 110–112; making friends with, 106–110, 112–113

Fay, Tropical Storm, 128–129

FEMA (Federal Emergency Management Agency), 40, 45–46, 171

Fire plugs, The, 30–31, 34, 45, 152

First Presbyterian Church, 154

Ford, Henry, 107

Fractals , 103

Funders, 31–32

Gabriel, Deborah, 155

Gabriel, Mark, 155

Galvanizers, The, 23

Gawande, Atul, 120

Giles, Dwight, 170

Givens, Scot, 71

Gladwell, Malcolm, 91, 171

Goins, Sheila, 34, 97

Golden, Arthur, 60

Grandparents Raising Grandchildren, 134

Granger, Greg, 62

Greater Baton Rouge Literacy Coalition, 147

Grimes, Blaine, 133

Haile, John, 70, 72, 79

Half horsepower man, 75–76, 79–80, 87

Half horsepower women, 79, 87

Handbook for Public Playground Safety, 160, 162, 169, 172

Hathaway, Lynn, 8, 11

Hayes, Woody, 18

Head Start, 147, 164

Head Start Body Start: the National Center for Physical Development and Outdoor Play, 161

Hemmerling, Bill, 90

Heroman, John, 76, 84

Howell, Joe, 13–16, 32, 40, 42, 53, 60, 66–79, 81, 87, 119–120, 155–156

Howell Park Elementary School, 60–67, 69, 71, 73, 74–80, 81–82, 86–87, 90, 109–110, 113, 124

Hudson, Patrice, 154

Idealist.org, 168

Integrity Recreation, 69, 71, 76

International Reading Association, 147, 173

Irvine, Betsy, 133, 140, 148

Jefferson Terrace Elementary School, 14, 71, 124

Jenkins, Georgia , 1–2, 5, 7, 9, 11

Jenkins, Woody, ix

Johnson, Lady Bird, 88

Jones, Jason, 173

KaBOOM! 34–35, 37, 72, 170

Katrina, Hurricane, 39, 44–45, 60–61, 110, 148, 172

Ketcham, Janet, 21, 128, 155

King Jr., Martin Luther, 32, 106

"King of the hill" (game) 3

"King of the surfacing pile" (game) 86

"King of the tire" (game) 3–4, 15, 83

Kissner, Elizabeth, 155

Kluger, Richard, 169

Knighten, Wayne, 76

Kohler, Kenny, 8–10, 38, 86

Koonce, Kenneth, 124

LaCEPT, 6, 12

Ladies, The, 9, 30–31, 37

Landrieu, Mary, ix

Landry, Henry, 156

Langlois, Mary, 61, 64–65

Learn and Serve America, 167

LeDuff, Lois, 6

Lennon, John, 86

Lewis, Cheryl, 113, 154

Lincoln, Abraham, 107

Loeb, Paul, 32, 100, 170

Louisiana School for the Deaf, 49–50

Louisiana State University (LSU), ix, 7, 29, 56, 61–64, 66–68, 71–74, 76, 80, 82, 102, 107–108, 149, 155

LSU Community Playground Project, x, 15, 16, 17, 19, 35, 36, 49, 60, 69, 74, 82, 88, 112, 154, 155

Martinez, Belinda, 10–11, 38, 86

Martinez, Robert, 38

McGuire, Saundra, 99

McMains Children's Developmental Center, 20–21, 127–128, 155

McMann, Casey, 82

Mead, Margaret, 134

Mensen, Kristin, 133

Merrydale Elementary School, 95

Microvolunteering, 137

Mississippi kite (bird), 77–79, 87

Mississippi State University, 70
Monroe, Marilyn, 107
Moore III, Pastor Alfred, 173
Morris, Brooke, 82, 84
MTV volunteer opportunities, 144
Murder rate, Baton Rouge, 80, 171
Murphy, Cindy, 21, 154

National Civilian Community Corps, 167
National Coalition for Literacy, 147, 173
National Institute of Health, 109–110
National Program for Playground Safety,
    159
National Public Radio, 156, 169
National Recreation and Park Association,
    160
National Science Foundation, 109
Newton's third law of motion, 55
Normand, Deborah, 21, 90, 133
Northwestern State University, 62–63

Obama, Barack, 65
Ohio State University, The, ix, 112
"Once in a While, a Protest Poem," 151
O'Neal, Shaquille, 56
O'Neil, Carol, 64
Our Lady of the Lake College (OLOL),
    73, 76
Oxfam America Hunger Banquet, 143

Pace, Janet, 133, 148
Parkview Elementary School, 54–55, 154
Patterson, James T., 169
Patterson, Ramona, 2
Penn State University, The, 82
Penny drive, 43–44
Play On!, 66

Playground safety surfacing, 5, 14, 32, 56,
    70, 161–162
Points of Light Institute, 167
Polk Elementary School, 56, 71
Porter, Tracy, 35, 90
Proposals (for funding), 5–6, 16, 28, 34, 40,
    61–65, 71, 87, 109–110, 113, 123, 136
Prothonotary warbler, 78
Provenza, Charlotte, 46
"Put out the fire" (game), 1–2, 4

Reardon, Ken, 100, 172
Reaves, Josh, 155
Remen, Rachel Naomi, 93
Renaissance Village, 44–46, 57, 170
Rideau, Harold, 45
Rita, Hurricane   39, 44
River Oaks Elementary School, 71, 124
Rodrigue, George, 90
Rosie O'Donnell Foundation, 46

Saints, New Orleans, 34–35, 90
Sansalone, Mary, 1
Schwindt, Angela, 36
Second law of thermodynamics,   55, 111
Seghers, Cindy, 133
SeniorCorps, 142, 167
Service-learning, ix, 33, 43, 62, 73, 107–109,
    150, 166, 167, 170
Shalley-Damburg, Marilyn, 173
Sharon Hills Elementary School, 72, 124
Shaw, George Bernard, 132
Shoemaker, Jan, 108, 116, 120, 133, 139, 150
*Simple Justice: The History of Brown v.
    Board of Education and Black America's
    Struggle for Equality*, 169
Simpson, Phyllis, 73, 77, 133, 149

Smith, Cas, 82

Smith, Julie, 71, 76

Soul of a Citizen: Living with Conviction in Challenging Times, 32, 170

Soul of the Community, 88–90, 97

South Boulevard Elementary School, 41–42, 90

Sparks, The, 19

Stagg, Karen, 133, 151

Stanley, Talmadge, 139, 145, 173

Stein, Gertrude, 107

Stone soup, 33, 88, 97–98, 100–102, 105

Sutter, Ford, 113–115, 121

Synergism, 37–38

Terrell, LeKeith, 66

Thompson, Willie, 76

Tipping Point, The, 91, 171

Trinity Christian Community, 148

Trochesset, Mallory, 133–134, 140, 143

Tsang, Edmund, 108

Tucker, Buddy, 173

Twin Oaks Elementary School, 52–54, 90, 104–105, 117–121

2.5 dimension, The, 103

U2, 97

Unitary surfacing material (USM), 127–128

United States Department of Agriculture (USDA), 65–66, 68, 71, 109

University of Louisiana System, 62

University of Michigan, 112

University of North Carolina at Chapel Hill, 82

University of South Florida, 143

University Terrace Elementary School, 33–34, 44, 71, 73, 101–102

University United Methodist Church, 34, 101

Villa del Rey Elementary School, 13–14, 16, 20, 38–40, 42, 44, 48, 71, 155

Virtual volunteering, 137

Volunteer Louisiana, 148

Volunteers in Public Schools, 101, 142, 172–173

Volunteers to Service in Americas (VISTA), 167

Walker, Nicole, 82

Wason, Melissa, 64

Westminister Elementary School, 71, 154

Where's the Learning in Service-Learning?, 170

Whicker, Caroline, 173

White Hills Elementary School, 113, 154

Wildwood Elementary School, 21, 154

Wilkinson, Larry, 173

Winfrey, Oprah, 65

Wyatt, Liz, 133

Yale Divinity School, 148

Yale University, 112

YK Coalition, 44, 46, 171

Young, Judy, 173

Zlotkowski, Edward, 107–108